Organize for Complexity
Niels Pflaeging

BetaCodex Publishing

Niels Pflaeging

ORGANIZE FOR COMPLEXITY

How to get life
back into work to build
the high-performance
organization

Revised edition with bonus chapter

BetaCodex Publishing, New York

The BetaCodex Publishing series:

Volume 1 – Niels Pflaeging: Organize for Complexity.
How to get life back into work to build the high-performance organization, 2014

Illustrations and cover design: Pia Steinmann, www.pia-steinmann.de
Copy editors: Deborah Hartmann Preuss, Paul Tolchinsky

Distributed in the US/Canada, UK/Europe, Australia and worldwide
by BetaCodex Publishing
ISBN 978-0-9915376-2-4

BetaCodex Publishing books are available at special discounts when purchased in bulk for events and sales promotions as well as for fund-raising or educational use. Special editions or book excerpts can also be created to specification. For details, send an e-mail to contact@nielspflaeging.com.

Version 1.2. - Deming

Visit us on the Internet: www.organizeforcomplexity.com,
www.betacodex.org, and www.nielspflaeging.com

"If you want to truly understand something, try to change it."

Kurt Lewin

Contents

How to use this book

You can read and use this book in a variety of ways.

As a textbook for thinking about organizations. It contains a selection of powerful thinking tools for dynamic-robust organization - all visualized and illustrated. Some of the concepts build on each other. So reading this book from front to back may be a good idea.

As a source of inspiration. You'll find ideas and suggestions for changing your organization. Your leadership work. Your team. Your clients' organizations.

As a dictionary. Organizing for complexity needs a new language; new terms; precise distinctions. Without appropriate terminology and vocabulary, we cannot conceive the organizational change needed for this age, let alone produce it. This book is packed with new and pointed terms. Those terms are often highlighted in the text, and sometimes set in brackets.

As a workbook. The book can serve you as a companion in change or transformation processes; individually, or for entire teams. Specific pieces of advice with regards to this can be found in particular in Chapters 5 to 7. At the end of the book, we added a few pages for your own personal notes.

{ Learn to fix the system, instead of fixing symptoms. }

The same questions, everywhere...

This book addresses fundamental questions of interest to business owners, managers, change agents and consultants, but also professionals of all kinds, in general.

Don't we all ask ourselves questions like:

- How can we adjust a growing organization, without falling into the bureaucracy trap?
- How can my organization deal with growing complexity?
- How can we become more capable of adapting to new circumstances?
- How can we overcome existing barriers to performance, innovation and growth?
- How can my firm achieve higher engagement and become an organization more fit to human beings overall?
- How can we produce profound change, without hitting a wall?

In this book, we argue that in order to address these issues, we must create and sustain organizations that are truly robust for complexity, as well as fit for human beings. We also discuss how that can be achieved.

{ You will learn to design your organization for complexity - regardless of size, age, industry, country or culture. }

Part 1

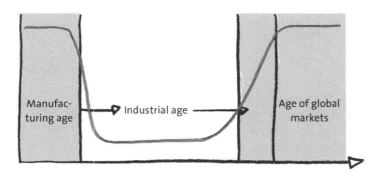

Manufac-
turing age

Industrial age

Age of global
markets

Complexity: Why it matters to work and organizations

(Big time.)

Management, the social technology: Rise and fall of a brilliant idea

"Thinkers"/Managers:
strategize, steer, control, decide

In 1911, Frederick W. Taylor published his landmark book "The Principles of Scientific Management." He proposed his new brand of organizational science as nothing short of a "revolution" that would eliminate the productivity constraints of the industrial-age organization. Taylorism indeed achieved just that. Taylor became the founder of management as an organizational method that would give wings to the quest for efficiency of the industrial age.

What Taylor pioneered was the idea of consistently dividing an organization between thinking people (managers) and executing people (workers) – thus legitimating the management profession as that of thinking principals of the non-thinking human resources. Taylor also introduced functional division to shop-floor work. His concepts were soon decried as inhumane and non-scientific, his consulting methods as ineffective. But Taylor was a visionary with the dream of pacifying workers and managers through efficiency gains that would benefit all.

"Doers"/Workers:
execute, obey, follow

The division principle became the DNA of management, the social technology: hierarchical and functional division were widely adopted after Taylor's death in 1915, and to great effect. His principles were later applied to non-industrial, non-shop-floor work - all kinds of work, in fact. Management, as we know it today, is not much different from what Taylor proposed a century ago. As we will see, however, command-and-control has turned toxic for both organizational performance and human/social advancement.

{ We call tayloristic management Alpha. }

The price of simplicity: Three systemic gaps caused by management

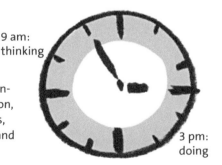

1. The Social Gap
Hierarchical division and top-down control cause an erosion of social/group pressure and dialog, and a bias towards management by numbers and leadership by fear

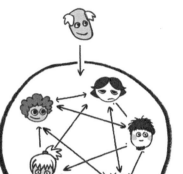

2. The Functional Gap
Functional division leads to narrow and fragmented responsibilities. It produces a need for managed/imposed coordination through process control, interfaces, planning, rules, standards, hierarchic power etc.

3. The Time Gap
The division between thinking thinkers and non-thinking doers, between planning and execution, results in the need for managed/imposed roles, complicated IT, strategy, targets, forecasting, and planning

9 am: thinking

3 pm: doing

{ None of this feels good. None of this creates value for people, customers, or owners: the three gaps all lead to waste. That´s a high price for the illusion of control. }

The historical course of market dynamics and the recent rise of complex, global markets

We call the graph shown on the right the "Taylor Bathtub."

The industrial age brought with it a brief period of fast-growing, spacious mass markets with relatively little competition. Monopolies or oligopolies dominated, markets were dull, or sluggish. During that period, Alpha became the standard organizational model: because it was possible, for the first time in human history, to largely eliminate complexity from value-creation with the help of machines and standards. For this task Taylorism, or Alpha, was the perfect solution.

Those days are gone. High-dynamic value creation re-emerged around the 70s, due to the rise of global, high-competition markets and the return of more individualized demand that made customization paramount and enabled "mass-customization."

High-dynamic value creation, in turn, calls for an increase in the human part of problem-solving processes. Alpha has become a roadblock.

* The terms dynamics and complexity will be used synonymously throughout this book, most of the time - for the sake of simplicity.

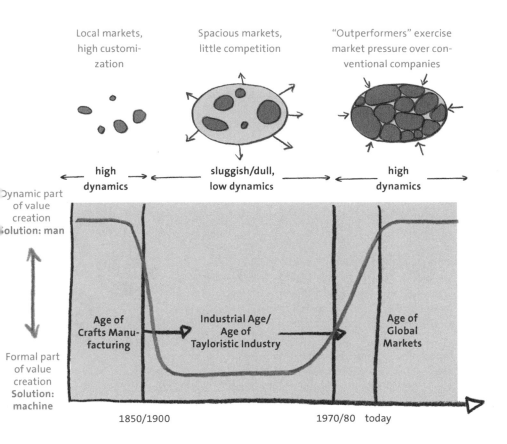

Local markets, high customization

Spacious markets, little competition

"Outperformers" exercise market pressure over conventional companies

high dynamics ← → sluggish/dull, low dynamics ← → high dynamics

Dynamic part of value creation
Solution: man

Formal part of value creation
Solution: machine

Age of Crafts Manufacturing

Industrial Age/ Age of Tayloristic Industry

Age of Global Markets

1850/1900

1970/80   today

{ The dominance of high dynamics and complexity is neither good, nor bad. It's a historical fact. }

The difference between
the complicated and the complex

Complicated systems operate in standardized ways. In complicated systems imprecision is diminished and non-objectivity and uncertainty are reduced as far as possible. Such a system can be described through non-ambiguous cause-and-effect chains. It is externally controllable.

Any high-precision machine is complicated: everything is done to avoid imprecision/to increase precision. A watch, for example, is calibrated to diminish mistakes and uncertainty. It is configured to supply objective data, certainty and a minimum of illusion.

Complex systems produce surprises. They have presence or participation of living creatures. They are living systems - that's why they may change at any moment. Such systems are only externally observable – not controllable.

A complex systems´ behavior is non-predictable. In a complex system, it's natural that there is a level of error, uncertainty and illusion that is much higher than in complicated systems. A complex system may possess elements that can operate in standardized ways, but their interaction would be constantly changing, in discontinuous ways.

{ To treat complex organizations as complicated systems is
a fundamental thinking mistake, an over-simplification. }

Consequences of complexity: The importance of mastery for problem-solving today

The only "thing" capable of dealing effectively with complexity is human beings.

What matters in complexity, as far as problem-solving is concerned, is neither tools, nor standardization, nor rules, nor structures, nor processes – all those things that used to serve us well in the industrial age and its dull markets.

In complexity, the question isn't how to solve a problem, but who can do it. What matters now is skillful people, or people with mastery or prowess. People with ideas. We call them professionals. Professionals who have pupils are called masters.

Problem-solving in a life-less system is about instruction. Problem-solving in a living system is about communication.

{ Complexity can be neither managed, nor reduced. We can only confront it with human mastery. }

The improvement paradox:
In complexity, working on separate parts doesn't improve the whole.
It actually damages the whole

Working on individual parts of the system does not improve the functioning of the whole: in a system it is not so much the parts that matter, but their fit.

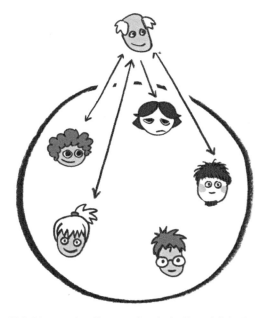

Thinking and acting mechanistically, additively

What really improves a system as a whole is working not on the parts itself, but on the inter-actions between the parts.
One might call this attitude "leadership."

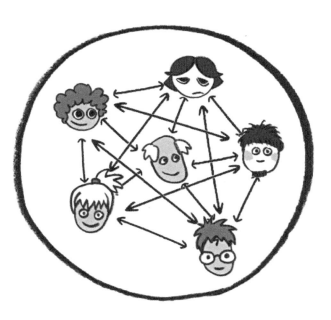

Thinking and acting systemically

{ Systems are not improved by tinkering with the parts, but by working on their interactions. }

Symptoms, or problems?
Not everything that looks
like a problem actually is one

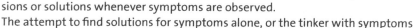

Most of the time when we
talk about "problems" in
the context of work and
organizations, we are not
actually discussing problems,
but rather symptoms. Symptoms
are the visible, touchable effects
of a problem. They include defects,
mistakes, bugs, or unpunctuality,
and resistance against change.

A simple thinking tool that helps to
"sharpen" problems, and to get to
the roots of problem´s symptoms,
is the "5 Whys" technique that
became famous through Toyota. It
prevents giving in to the tempta-
tion of hastily jumping to conclu-
sions or solutions whenever symptoms are observed.
The attempt to find solutions for symptoms alone, or the tinker with symptoms
before the problem has been understood, is called activism.

In complexity problems´ complex portions tend to be connected, forming messes.
Because of this individual problems often cannot be solved in an isolated fashion.
Just as an uncountable number of water lily leaves may cover a lake´s surface - all
coming from only one or a few plants rooted in the bottom of the lake. In organizations, you may find hundreds of problem symptoms, but only a handful problems
which may go back to one or two messes. By acting upon the messes with ad-
equately complex solutions, many problems dissolve.
Tools are unsuitable to deal with messes.

{ Activism breeds failure and makes learning impossible. }

Consequences of complexity: The importance of mastering problem-solving in dynamic contexts

In sluggish markets, organizational success was produced by applying Alpha methods and behavioral repertoires. Therefore, people in many organizations know and command just this one kind of repertoire. It is similar to having been raised in England and being used to driving on the left side of traffic.

We tend to ascribe experienced success to our own behavioral repertoire: "I was successful because I acted so and so." In fact, we were successful because the behavior matched the context.

Today, in high dynamics, success demands another repertoire, one that is appropriate to this new context, but also one that has hardly been practiced or learned. This new repertoire may even be ridiculed. Then they say: "Soft skills are for people who don't know anything else," or, "That's a nice-to-have, but not performance-relevant." Failure is ascribed to changes in context, but not our own behavior. So organizations today tend to deal badly with problems by reflex. It is like driving a car in England after having just arrived.

{ We must re-train our reflexes. }

Part 2

Humans at work:
The secret ingredient

(How to fulfill and capture
human potential)

The working human:
McGregor's insightful distinction

Ask yourself: which of these theories describes me,
which describes the people around me?

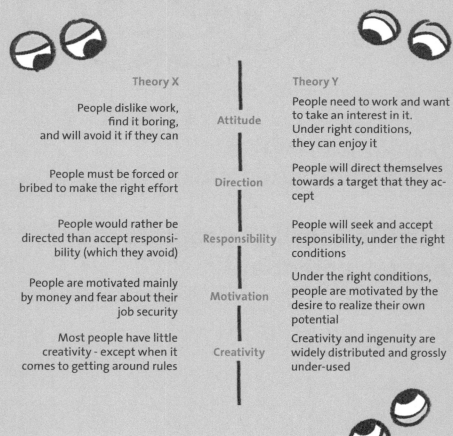

	Theory X		Theory Y
Attitude	People dislike work, find it boring, and will avoid it if they can		People need to work and want to take an interest in it. Under right conditions, they can enjoy it
Direction	People must be forced or bribed to make the right effort		People will direct themselves towards a target that they accept
Responsibility	People would rather be directed than accept responsibility (which they avoid)		People will seek and accept responsibility, under the right conditions
Motivation	People are motivated mainly by money and fear about their job security		Under the right conditions, people are motivated by the desire to realize their own potential
Creativity	Most people have little creativity - except when it comes to getting around rules		Creativity and ingenuity are widely distributed and grossly under-used

After Douglas McGregor, The Human Side of the Enterprise, 1960

Human nature at work:
We have an observation problem

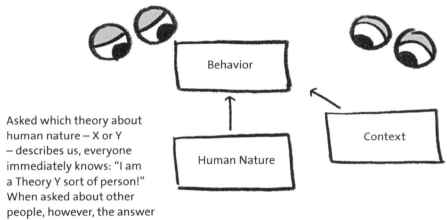

Asked which theory about human nature – X or Y – describes us, everyone immediately knows: "I am a Theory Y sort of person!" When asked about other people, however, the answer is usually not as clear cut. Haven't we all experienced Theory X people many times in our lives? At work? In our organizations?

Douglas McGregor, in his seminal work from 1960, distinguished between two images of human nature, of which only one is "true", in that it holds up to science and available theory. The other one, Theory X, is nothing more than a prejudice that we have about other people. There are two reasons why Theory X thinking is still commonplace, in spite of being superstitious. Firstly, it reflects common thinking from our pre-democratic, pre-enlightenment past. Secondly, while observing other people's behavior, we tend to make conclusions about their human nature – frequently ignoring behavior-shaping context. We call the result naive cynicism.

This matters. It matters because assumptions we have about other people shape our behavior, and the way we tend to design and run organizations. If you believe in the existence of Theory X humans, then command-and-control systems design will follow. In order to build complexity-robust organizations, a shared, enlightened and refined view of human nature is needed.

{ We cannot act on systems, leadership, performance, or change coherently if we don´t agree beforehand on the assumptions we hold about human nature. }

The nature of motivation –
and why leaders cannot motivate

People are driven by motives. It is safe to say that everyone carries all kinds of motives. Everyone thus is a "carrier of motives", or "intrinsically motivated." The specific levels or the dominance of the various motives, however, vary greatly among individuals.

What this means for organizations, or employers, is: they cannot motivate. Because motivation *is*. The main thing that organizations can do to stimulate performance is facilitating options for connection between individuals and throughout the organization, through purpose and meaningful work. We call the phenomenon, when an individual connects voluntarily to work and an organization, connectedness.

Unfortunately, belief in the myth of motivational power of leaders is still widespread. The truth is: because of motivation's intrinsic nature, leaders, through their behavior, can only de-motivate, or at best create the context for motivation to show up.

{ Any attempt to motivate can only lead to de-motivation. }

Most familiar management tools and organizational practices are ineffective or outright damaging

Management thinker Peter Drucker once wrote that 90% of the practices that we call management do nothing more than keep people from their work.

One might argue about the exact percentage, but Drucker was right with his conclusion, overall. The question remains, however, which are these 90%?

McGregor´s distinction is highly useful for responding to this question: all practices that are based on Theory X assumptions and designed for "X people" must be ineffective or even dangerous. Here are a few examples.

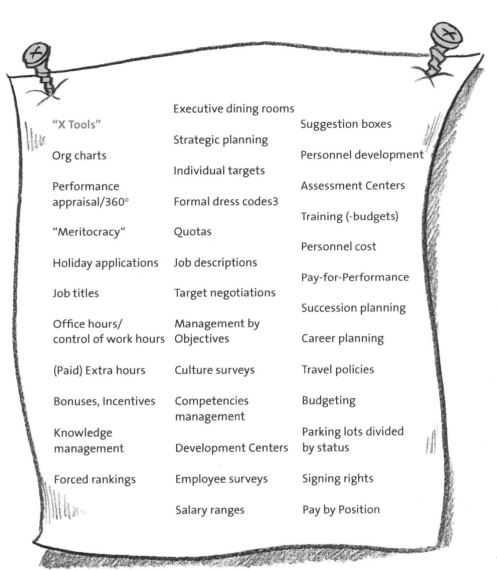

"X Tools"	Executive dining rooms	Suggestion boxes
Org charts	Strategic planning	Personnel development
Performance appraisal/360°	Individual targets	Assessment Centers
"Meritocracy"	Formal dress codes3	Training (-budgets)
	Quotas	Personnel cost
Holiday applications	Job descriptions	Pay-for-Performance
Job titles	Target negotiations	Succession planning
Office hours/ control of work hours	Management by Objectives	Career planning
(Paid) Extra hours	Culture surveys	Travel policies
Bonuses, Incentives	Competencies management	Budgeting
Knowledge management	Development Centers	Parking lots divided by status
Forced rankings	Employee surveys	Signing rights
	Salary ranges	Pay by Position

{ Tools and practices can be tested by asking: Upon what assumptions about human nature are they based - Theory X or Theory Y? }

Appreciating behavioral distinctiveness: People and preferences

An individual's behavior is also strongly influenced by preferences. The concept of "preferences" was introduced by Carl G. Jung in his pioneering work "Psychological Types."

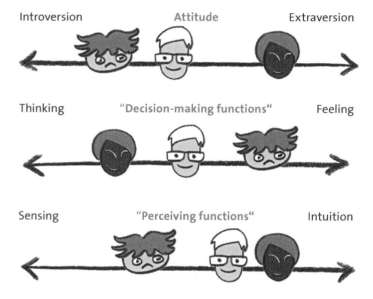

Introversion   Attitude   Extraversion

Thinking   "Decision-making functions"   Feeling

Sensing   "Perceiving functions"   Intuition

Attitude. Jung differentiated types firstly according to their general attitude. Attitude describes people's tendency to react more to outer or inner experiences.

"Decision-making functions." 'Heady' individuals, who prefer to make decisions by thinking things through, rationally using the 'thinking function'. 'Heart' people prefer to evaluate and make decisions subjectively using the 'feeling' function.

"Perceiving functions." We view the world using a combination of 'sensing' to record the sensory details, and 'intuition' to see patterns, make connections and interpret meaning starting from the big picture.

Making use of differences in preference to deal with complexity

There is a great variety of behavior within the three categories of preferences, depending on where on each of the three bipolar scales the person's behavior is plotted. The majority of people will not be extreme, but nearly balanced; as such they can be more difficult to read.

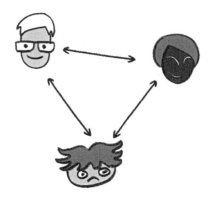

Every person has the ability to use either side of the bipolar scales, although we all have preferences for one side more than the other – most of the time.

When people with different preferences work together, they can compliment each other.

{ In complexity, diversity in motivations and preferences can be an asset, or a liability, depending on the level of self-reflection present. }

The complexity of human individuality: an overview

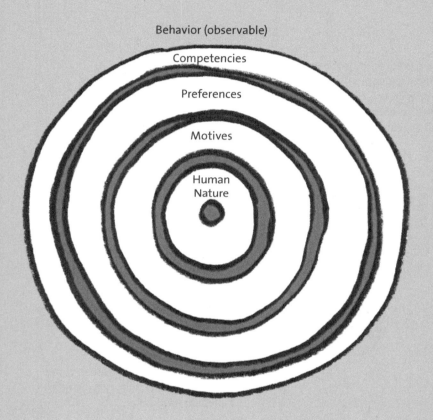

Behavior (observable)

Competencies

Preferences

Motives

Human Nature

An individual's behavior is shaped by motives, preferences and competencies. Motives are quite stable over time – they describe how important certain goals are for the individual. Preferences, by contrast, can evolve somewhat during the course of a lifetime - depending on environment, challenges and personal goals.

Motives and preferences, combined, influence our interest to acquire certain competencies: abilities are either present or can be obtained. Competencies, thus, are directly related to learning.

As we have seen, only behavior is easily and readily observable. It is also relatively easy to describe an individual's competencies. With a little more effort yet, preferences can be mapped and described. Proper identification of someone's motives requires even more effort and delicacy. Human nature, itself, cannot be observed at all: it is a matter of conviction, or part of the social constructs that we hold.

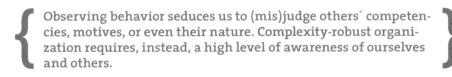

{ Observing behavior seduces us to (mis)judge others´ competencies, motives, or even their nature. Complexity-robust organization requires, instead, a high level of awareness of ourselves and others. }

Individual competence vs. collective competence

"We learned that individual expertise did not distinguish people as high performers. What distinguished high performers were larger and more diversified personal networks."

"Engineers are roughly five times more likely to turn to a person for information than to an impersonal source such as a database."

Cross, Rob et. al.The Hidden Power of Social Networks.
Boston: Harvard Business School Press, 2004

Many organizations are obsessed with personal results. But individual performance is actually a myth

Individual performance is not just overrated. In organizations, it simply doesn't exist.

Why? Because value, or results, never arise from individual action, but from interaction between various individuals, or within teams. A sales person only does part of the sale – the other parts are being done by people who may call themselves back office staff, production and procurement staff, accountants and HR professionals.

Which also means that individual competencies and skills are of relatively little importance for an organization. It is the collective applied competencies and abilities in the system that make the difference.

Because interdependency is ubiquitous in organizations, trying to define individual targets, or to measure individual performance, leads to deception.

{ Appraisal of "individual" performance can only have a de-spiriting and de-motivating effect on people and damages team spirit. }

People communicate & connect in wildly different manners: About the archetypes of communicators

Hubs
draw information and broadcast it

Gatekeepers
carefully manage information flows

Pulsetakers
great observers of people

Karen Stephenson, Quantum Theory of Trust.
Harlow: Pearson Education Ltd, 2005

Connectors
prefer to exchange information with many people

Mavens
Information broker/specialists who feel an urge to share

Salesmen
Masters in convincing and negotiating

Malcolm Gladwell, The Tipping Point.
Boston: Back Bay Books, 2002

{ It is not important which of these models is "true" or "better":
They offer a huge advantage in understanding social patterns
and varied ways of acting. Make use of them, or ignore them at
your peril. }

The learning riddle:
Data and information
don't make smarts

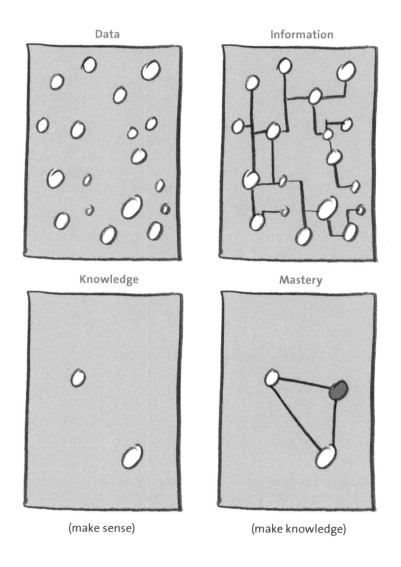

Data   Information

Knowledge   Mastery

(make sense)   (make knowledge)

Through contextualization, data can be transformed into information. Both data and information are inert: they can be stored and are both independent of human carriers.

Knowledge is different: it requires human assimilation, or learning. Study, experience and being taught are learning enablers. Knowledge can be applied to known problems by those who have learned skills or developed expertise.

Mastery is the human capability to solve new problems. It can only be developed through practice. We call this "disciplined practice."

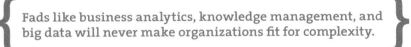

{ Fads like business analytics, knowledge management, and big data will never make organizations fit for complexity. }

Part 3

Self-organizing teams
and the networked organization

(From old design principles
to new and better ones)

Forming teams:
The phenomenon of chunking

"The idea of 'chunking': a group of items is perceived as a single 'chunk.' The chunk's boundary is a little like a cell membrane or a national border. It establishes a separate identity for the cluster within. According to context, one may wish to ignore the chunk's internal structure or take it into account."

Hofstädter/Douglas, Gödel, Escher, Bach.
New York: Basic Books, 1979

{ We call the individual chunk a cell,
and the chunk's boundary the cell membrane. }

{ We call the cluster of cells (the system),
a cell-structure network. }

{ We call the system's boundary or membrane
the Sphere of Activity. }

Organizing the work: Common forms of chunking – and where the difference lies

Design principle *Beta* – following the work:
Teams are multi-functional, interdisciplinary, or functionally integrated. "Diverse individuals who work in an inter-connected fashion, with each other and for each other"- individuals who commit to work together to reach a common goal.

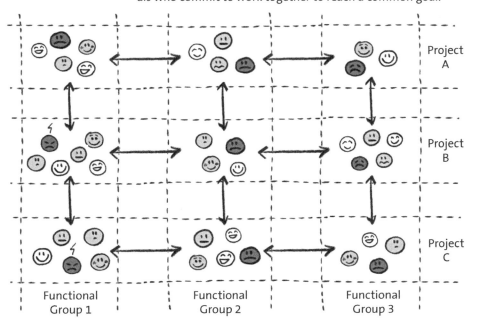

Design principle *Alpha* – following functions:
Groups are uni-functional, or functionally differentiated.
"Similar Individuals who work next to each other, in parallel", eventually competing against each other

{ "Team" and "Group" are two different concepts, entirely. }

35

Top-down command-and-control versus self-organization

Design principle *Alpha*:

Control through bosses. Information flows up, commands flow down. Top-down decision-making. Use of rules for containment and compliance.

Design principle *Beta*:

Self-regulation within the team. Control through peer pressure and transparency. Principles and shared responsibility.

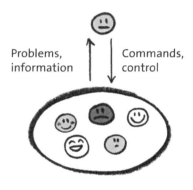

Problems, information | Commands, control

Radical transparency, social density, group pressure

Boundary: rules, responsibilities, job descriptions

Boundary: values, principles, roles, shared external objectives

{ Self-organization is not the "right" term.
Better would be: Socially dense market-organization. }

Making use of social pressure

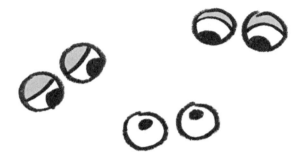

This is how "social pressure", or "group pressure"
is produced:

1. Let people identify with a small group.

2. Give them shared responsibility for shared goals.

3. Make all information open and transparent to the team.

4. Make performance information comparable across teams.

{ Social pressure, used correctly: far more powerful
than hierarchy, no damaging side-effects. }

Self-organization must be team-based

Ultimately, organizing for complexity and self-organization are always about empowering teams...

... not about empowering individuals

{ The empowerment movement of the 1990´s missed this point. }

A seeming paradox: Giving up power and decentralizing decision-making to teams increases status

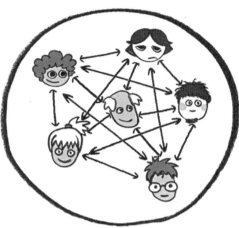

High, or superior performance

Low, or average performance

{ Success is not a zero-sum game. }

Communication across teams

Design principle *Alpha:*
Coordination/communication through a manager, usually combined
with functional division; taylorism.
This is sufficient in dull markets.

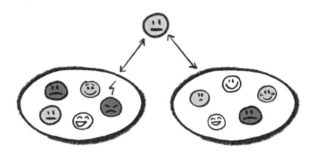

Design principle *Beta:*
Coordination/communication not through a manager, but later-
ally, usually combined with market-like mechanisms.
This is superior and more potent in dynamic markets.

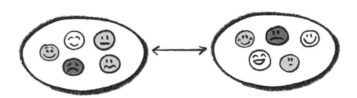

{ Centralized coordination is a luxury organizations in
complex markets cannot afford. }

The difference between a "department" and a "cell"

Design principle *Alpha*:
A department implies functional differentiation and thus the grouping of functional specialists - marketers with marketers, sales people with sales people, etc. - all of which have to be coordinated vertically and horizontally. Business processes cross multiple departments. Result: groups of people working in parallel, not as teams

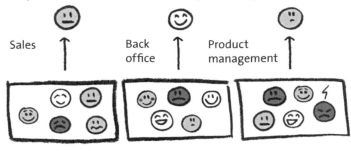

Design principle *Beta*:
A cell implies functional integration, or cross-functional teams - so the same functions can be encountered in different teams. Coordination occurs laterally, among peers. Communication between teams is peer-to-peer. Business processes flow mainly within teams. Result: actual teams of people working for and with each other

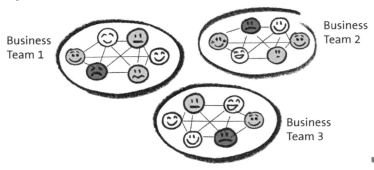

{ Complex markets require decentralization, combined with market-like coordination. }

41

Part4

Organizations as systems: Designing for complexity

(How any organization can become "fit for dynamics")

The problem of the dominant mind-set: To imagine organizations as pyramids is a misguided metaphor

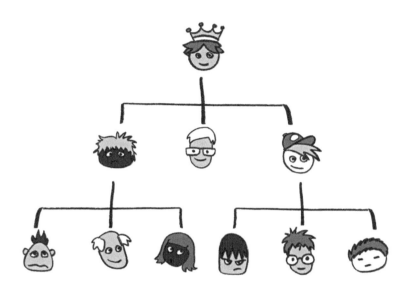

Design principle *Alpha*:
The organization as a bureaucratic hierarchy, steered by managers who are always in control.
Managers commanding/controlling a pyramid of "followers" from above is not a smart way to organize. **The problem is with the boxes *and* with the wiring.** Most of us sense that, intuitively: Our experience from practice contradicts the assertion that this kind of "leadership" can actually work.

This remains, however, the dominant mindset in companies, ever since the development of management theory about a century ago. When we speak of "management", we usually refer to techniques, tools and models aimed at improving, optimizing, or fixing organizations as command-and-control pyramids.

A better metaphor: Organizations as multi-layered networks

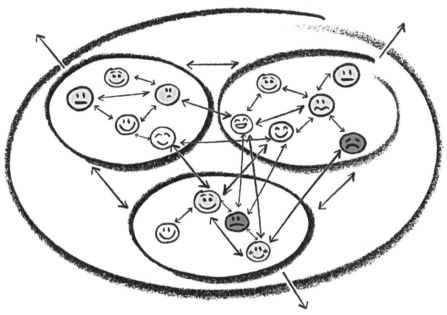

Design principle *Beta*:
The organization as an inter-connected, living network, steered by market forces. Nobody is in control. Everybody is in charge.

A smarter and more useful way to look at organizations is to see them as networks. This is more aligned with contemporary thinking than the mechanistic "pyramid" dogma, and it is also far closer to reality, in several ways. Organizations are, in fact:
• Networks of individuals (through Informal structure) and
• Networks of value-creating teams (through Value Creation structure).
Let's take a closer look at these concepts.

{ Your organization is already networked.
It is just not allowed to officially operate as one. }

The work is networked: Informal structure, based on social relationships

Informal Structures emerge out of human interaction. This happens in any social group. In crisis, especially, the unofficial collegial networks take over. The informal shortcut then shows its superiority, compared with official, pre-described processes that are actually junk.

Informal Structure by itself is neither good nor bad. It simply is. Most social phenomena arise from informal structure: Gossip. Networking. Socializing. Politics. Groupthink. Conspiracies. Factions, coalitions and clans. Resistance to change. Peer pressure. Solidarity. Bullying. You name it.

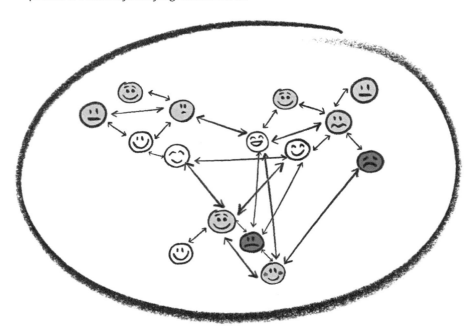

{ Informal structures are powerful. Every organization has them. }

The key to survival - also networked:
Value Creation structure,
based on team interaction

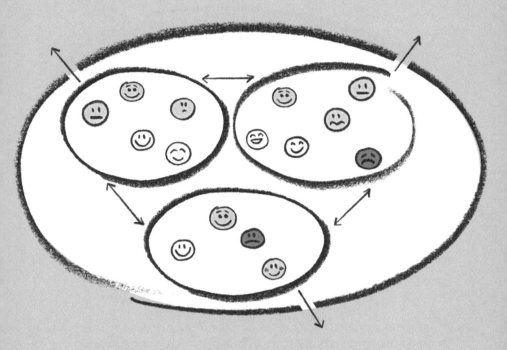

In an organization value-creation flows from the inside-out.

Value creation is never the result of individual action, but of inter-action: It is a team-based process of working "with-one-another-for-each-other."
Any organization, even the most ineffective and bureaucratic, has a value creation structure. It may be hidden or little-known, though. And even the language to describe it may be lacking.

{
   In hierarchically managed organization, value-creation structure
   is immobilized. Like a muscle stunned by anesthetic injection.
}

The work is doubly networked: Bringing together Informal and Value Creation structures

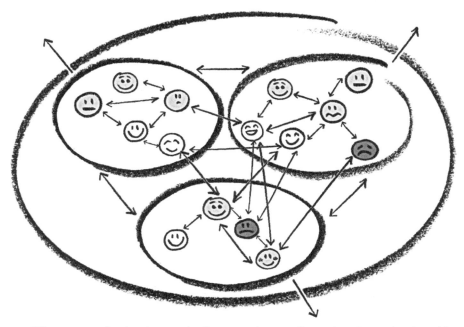

When one understands organizations as value creation networks, underpinned by informal structures, and not as command-and-control pyramids, one will stop caring much about formal hierarchy (which is actually "trivial", from the point of view of complexity thinking and can only provide for external compliance).

Instead, one will care a great deal about value creation streams, about supporting peer pressure and emergent networking patterns. Organizational robustness, here, comes from the quality and quantity of the inter-connections between humans and teams – not from rules, bosses, or standards.

{ Informal and Value Creation structures constitute
the backstage of any organization. }

However, to understand value creation, it is helpful to distinguish between center and periphery

Through the distinction between center and periphery, dynamics problems become observable that would remain invisible (and thus unsolvable) using common distinctions such as between functional and divisional structure, line and process organization, strategic and operational.

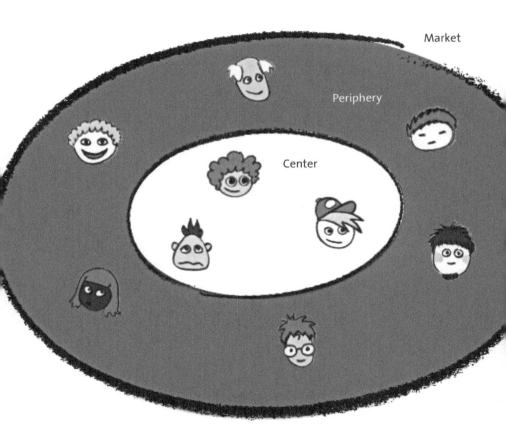

The periphery: The outer portion of the organization

We call all roles dealing with requirements of the external market in a value-creating way periphery.

{ The periphery is the only part of an organization with market contact. Through this interaction, the periphery is capable of learning from the market. }

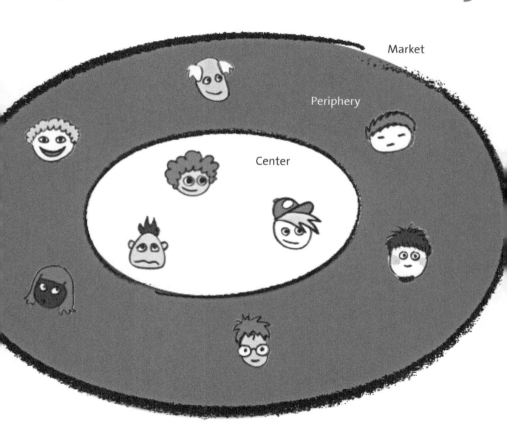

Market

Periphery

Center

The center:
Deprived of direct market contact

The periphery isolates the center from the market. But caution: A board of directors and corporate headquarters are not the same as the center. Workers at plants, employees at branches or offices are not to be equated with the periphery. This distinction is about roles or activities - not about individual people, places or locations.

Innovation is always carried out by the center. Because innovation is not (yet) immediate client value creation. Those dealing with innovation in an organization thus always play a role of the center. They put on a central hat, so to say.

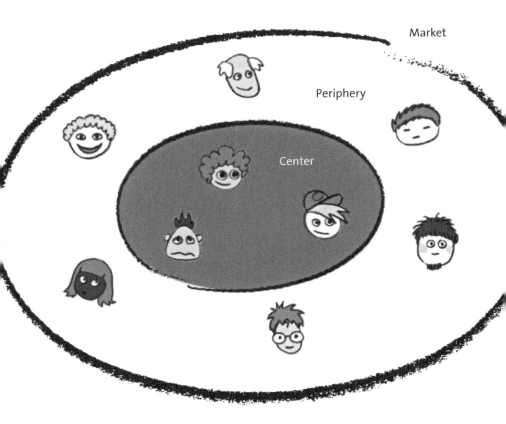

Centralized decision-making and steering (command-and-control), from a systems perspective

Design principle *Alpha*: Centralized decision-making, internal steering, command-and-control

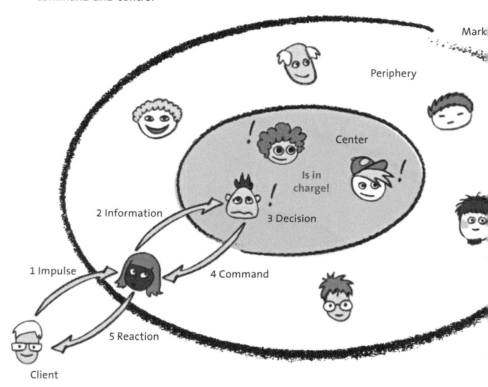

In dull, slow-moving markets, centralization of decision-making is efficient. The centre solves problems and gives out orders – the periphery executes upon them. Centralized control is obtainable. Standards work. In fast-moving markets, however, the centre loses its knowledge superiority: Central steering and any system that re- lies on central decisions collapses. Such systems become dumbed-down and numb.

Solving the complexity dilemma through decentralization

Design principle *Beta*: Decentralized decision-making, sense-and-respond

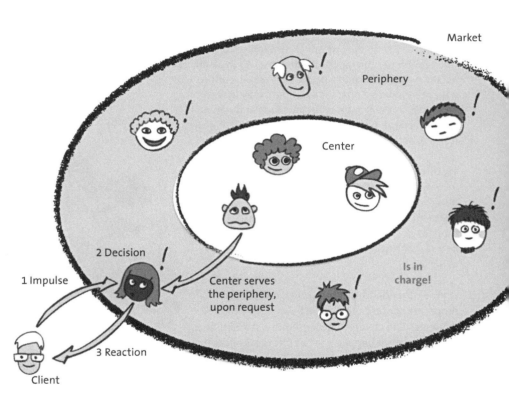

Market

Periphery

Center

2 Decision

1 Impulse

Is in charge!

Center serves the periphery, upon request

3 Reaction

Client

In dynamic markets the way out of the control dilemma is consequent decentralization, or devolution of decision-making, which becomes far more effective: This way decisions are taken where interaction with - and learning from - the market occurs. The roles of both center and periphery change dramatically, compared to Alpha.

A few words about culture:
Why culture is like a shadow

Culture is not a success factor, but an effect of success or failure. It is an image of the circumstances in an organization, not their cause. That is why it also cannot be influenced directly. Culture is like a shadow.

Culture is observable but not controllable. Cultural development is neither difficult nor a problem - it happens all the time. All by itself. But cultural development projects can only fail. And to demand a certain culture - a more innovative one, for example - may indeed be common, but will always be ridiculous and remain a hollow appeal: A company cannot choose its culture, it has exactly the culture it deserves.

Culture is something like the restless memory of an organization. It facilitates or prevents deviant behavior. It does not standardize - no one has to be obedient to it! But it endows something like a common "style" which all can rely on. Culture thus acts as a simplification mechanism and is conservative in nature.

On the other hand, organizational culture also processes contradictions that arise from external dynamics and change. Like a memory, it assimilates everything that happens. What it forgets and what not, that again is not controllable. Culture, in this sense, is autonomous.

{ Culture neither is a barrier to change, nor does it encourage change. It can provide hints to what an organization must learn. }

To change culture is impossible, but culture observation is valuable

Large companies often try to work on their culture and values. If anything, these activities can only impact behavior. Values, however - another mechanism of organizational memory - do not follow rational considerations, and thus remain unaffected by attempts at controlling them. Or they may even be adversely affected, because such activism often breeds hypocrisy.

Culture observation is an essential tool for change and organizational development. Culture is an unbeatable sensor for the effectiveness of change efforts. Employee surveys, on the other hand, are useless for cultural observation (and in general), because they can only capture individual opinion. Behavior and other, invisible, phenomena such as values, and informal structures, or the backstage of an organization, remain hidden to this kind of method.

The visible parts of culture, its symptoms, only become observable in practice: in behavior and communication. Through sick leave, in the design of offices and workplaces, in the number of e-mails and secure copies, in error rates and customer complaints, in the design and use of media and communication tools, indicators and reports. Interviews and, in particular, "learning, chained interviews" are another proven tool for cultural observation that can be applied by an external change agent.

{ Culture allows us to indirectly observe the quality of change efforts: Change trickles through into the culture. }

Delegate, or decentralize?

Decentralization goes further than delegation. While delegation occurs at an individual level, when a superior decides to pass on a power or responsibility or task to a subordinate, decentralization occurs when a board of directors (or equivalent) decides as a policy to pass on power to peripheral parts of an organization.

Ultimately, decentralization goes along with structural changes that impart a greater degree of autonomy (Greek: self governance), mainly through functional integration within teams.

Decentralization will usually also involve decentralizing activities, in order to provide teams with greater autonomy. But this does not mean that all activities must be decentralized. Activities may be centralized or decentralized. The important issue is how interacting teams are connected.

Delegation   Decentralization

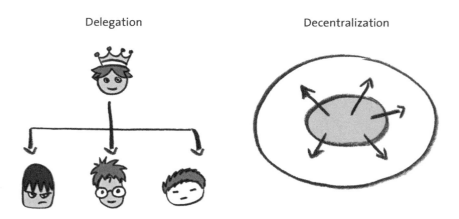

{ Decentralization is more permanent than delegation. It is principled; it must be wired into structure and value-creation. }

Part 5

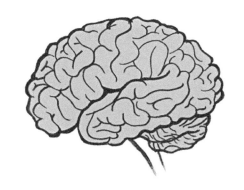

Dynamic-robust networks for all:
This is how you pull it off

(How to anchor the "Beta" mindset
within organizational structure)

Designing an organization as a decentralized network - not as a command-and-control pyramid

To turn your organization into a decentralized cell-structure, or to build a new organization as such a network, one must understand the elements, or components, of such a design.

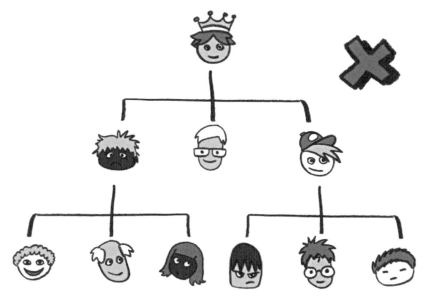

Four construction elements are required:
*   an organizational boundary, or sphere of activity, that sets the limits of action
*   network cells - with a distinction between central and peripheral cells
*   connections between these network cells, and finally,
*   market contact, or steering, through connections with the external market

{ No line structures. No functions. No departments. No shared services. No divisions. No centralized staff. This is a different, and far more effective way of defining structure in complexity. }

Identity and the Sphere of Activity: The difference between inside and outside

Sphere of Activity

- Business model
- (shared) Values
- Principles
- Brand proposal
- Rituals
- "Memes"
- ...

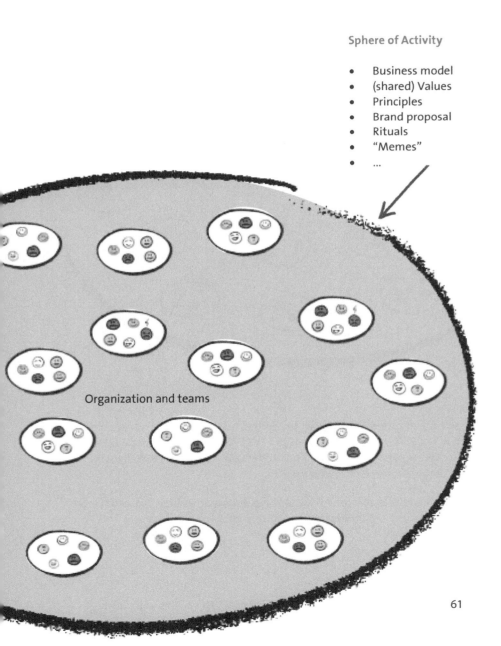

Organization and teams

The Sphere of Activity

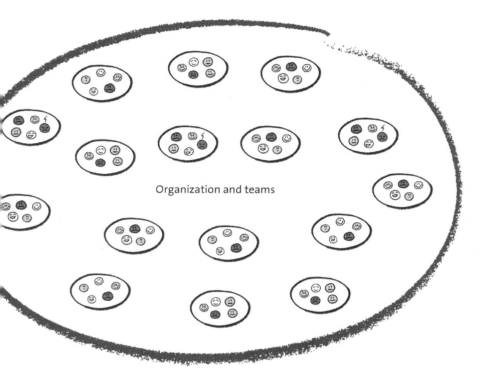

Organization and teams

Self-organization requires that the system is surrounded by a containing boundary. **This condition defines the "self" that will be developed during the self-organizing process.** The containing boundary serves to direct self-organization towards value-creation.

The elements of this sphere should be put down in writing, e.g. in a "Letter to Ourselves", a "Manifesto" or a "Culture Book."

The market and its components

Market

- Customers
- Owners
- Banks
- Society
- Competitors
- Suppliers
- Unions
- Research institutions
- ...

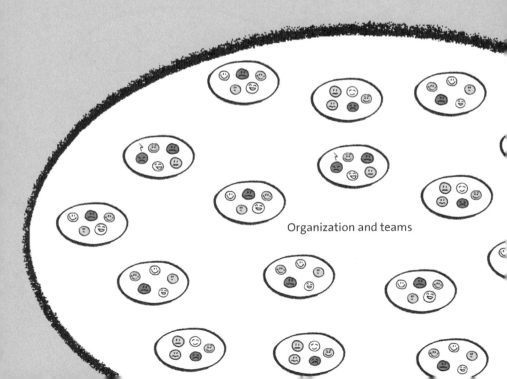

Organization and teams

Value-creation flows from the inside out. Market-pull provides the steering

A cell-structure network gains stability and resilience not through hierarchical power relationships, or through "resistance to pressure", but through the "pull" that comes from the external market, and from the complex human relationships it nourishes internally. Market dynamics do the steering.

Sounds simple? It is.

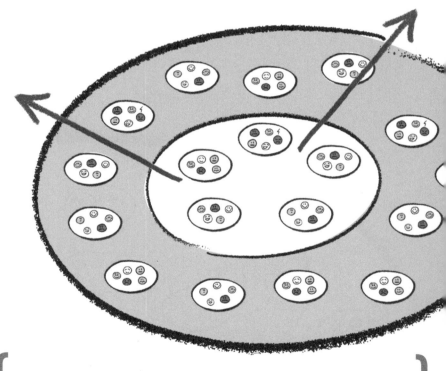

{ Organizations outsourced the steering to markets a long time ago. }

From "value-creating teams" to "value-creating network"

{ We call the links between individual network cells strings. }

{ We call the links between peripheral cells and the market, i.e. where the system interrelates with the market, market pull. }

Through market pull and strings, tension is applied within the organization and between cells.

Only peripheral cells have direct links to the market and can thus deliver value externally.

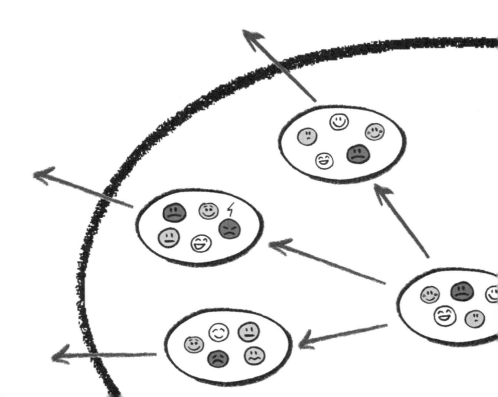

The "market pull" phenomenon

Market pull is what connects the market with the organization. Whenever an external stakeholder of an organization "wants" or "demands", "orders" or does something relevant to the organization, this will initiate market pull.

Market pull can be caused by customers wanting something, by shareholders demanding a compensation for their investment, a bank demanding payback of a loan, the state demanding the payment of taxes, or a competitor launching a new product. Market pull thus has varied sources.

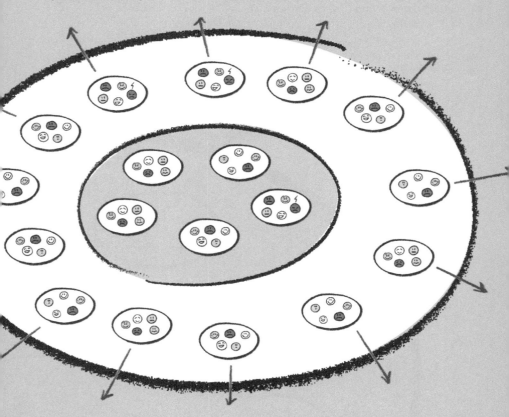

Drafting your organization as a value-flow network. Step 1: Start from the outside-in

Start from the market inwards, and thus by thinking about peripheral cells first.

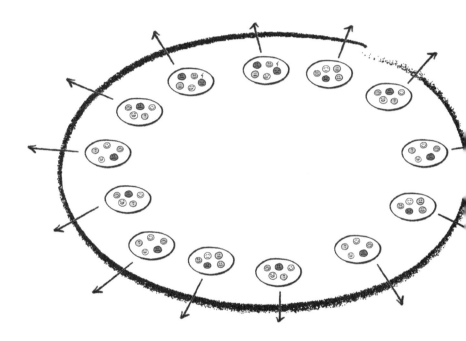

Peripheral cells should:

- be as autonomous as possible in their decision-making, functioning like "mini-enterprises", responsible for individual businesses, holistically
- contain no less than three team members each, with cross-functional capacities and roles
- measure their own results.

Step 2: Design central cells as internal supply units - with no decision-making power over the periphery

The role of central cells is to deliver value to peripheral teams that they cannot create for themselves. Their role is to serve, not to rule, the periphery. It is not to execute decision-making power, nor to steer or control.

Ideally, these teams sell their services to peripheral cells on an as-used basis, through priced transactions, and on an internal market. For this, definitions of internal services and prices are necessary, but fixing purchase quantities must be avoided. Examples of how to do this consistently exist at companies such as Handelsbanken, dm-drogerie markt, and Morning Star.

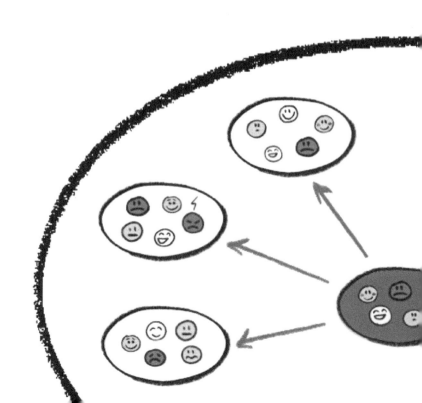

The roles of central network cells

Central services might fall into the following categories:
- Personnel/Human Resources
- Finance
- Systems administration (IT)
- Legal
- other centers of expertise

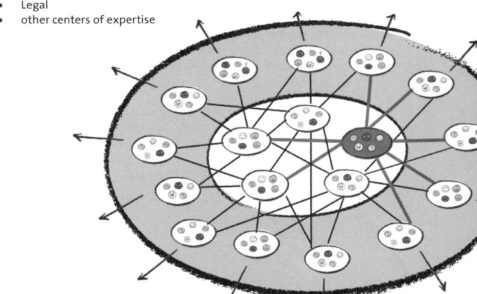

There need not be one cell per category, of course. In smaller organizations, combining internal services in one or two central "shops" or "supermarkets" can suffice.

A model with two "shops" may look like this:
- "Org Shop" – a team delivering organizational services for the whole network, such as HR, legal, administrative
- "Info Shop" - a team delivering services related to information systems and supply, such as finance and IT

Step 3: Iterate.
Involve many people in the process of designing a full network structure

People involved in the process of deciding what the changes should be are transformed by the process. Those who are not involved are not transformed and may never be.

Usually, you will have to go through a few iterations to arrive at a value-structure design that is not only better than the previous formal structure, but also as decentralized as possible, scalable and viable in the long-term. More often than not, an organization will make adjustments after some initial learning with the new design. This can lead to frequent improvements on the structure.

{ Generally speaking, the more organization members are involved in the design-finding process, the better the result. }

Cultivate principles, not rules

Complicated/many rules
> stupid behavior

IF ..... THEN .....
IF ..... THEN .....
IF ..... THEN .....
IF ..... THEN .....
IF ..... THEN .....
IF ..... THEN .....
IF ..... THEN .....
IF ..... THEN .....
IF ..... THEN .....
IF ..... THEN .....
IF ..... THEN .....
IF ..... THEN .....
IF ..... THEN .....
IF ..... THEN .....
IF ..... THEN .....
IF ..... THEN .....
IF ..... THEN .....

Simple/few principles
> complex behavior

DON'T DO EVIL.

Individuals and their "portfolios of roles": A basic feature of decentralized network structures

In a decentralized network structure, "positions" cease to exist. "Roles" rule. Individuals usually are not confined to one role, or one network cell alone, but will act in different cells, filling in different roles in different parts of the network. Consequently, everyone keeps "juggling roles", all the time.

An example: Someone with the official title of "CFO" on the business card would play a role in a central cell when serving other teams of the network, but be part of a peripheral cell when dealing with a bank. The same person might also fulfill additional roles within the organization that might have little or nothing to do with finance.

{ In a cell structure, roles can change frequently and formal status becomes less important. Members of an organization will not be pressed into job descriptions - they build individual role portfolios of their own. }

Roles, not positions:
Multiple scopes, more colorful
work-life. Learning: enabled

Newcomer	Moderator	Sales	Accountant	Expert	Recruiter
Cultural Icon	Idea Donor	Information Provider	Maverick	General Manager	Master
Developer	Marketer	Organization Folklorist	HR	Task Force Member	Market Researcher
Auditor	Specialist	Visitor Tour Guide	CEO	Negotiation Leader	Proposal Writer
Administrator	Internal Client	Quality Officer	Treasurer	Team Speaker	Me

Part6

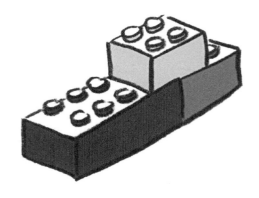

Leadership in complexity: What remains of it, and what is needed

(Practical recommendations for dynamic-robust leadership work)

Leadership as leading employees: If only it were so easy!

In his book "Change or Die", business writer Alan Deutschman draws upon insights from scientific research from a variety of spheres of life to illustrate what it takes to nudge people towards personal change - and what does not do the job. Deutschman distinguishes between the "Three Fs" and the "Three Rs."

The "Three Fs" – practiced, known (and unfit):

Facts: "Hard facts speak logically for themselves."

Fear: "Fear of consequences provides the emotional boost."

Force: "Pressure through formal power, control or incentives ensures success."

Applying the "Three Fs" leads safely to a few direct consequences: Distress, discouragement, frustration. Such a mechanistic approach to change ultimately results in behavioral control and conditioning; to repressing employees, but not to learning.

The "Three Fs" are typical of hierarchical leadership, based on formal power relations, or command and control. They are also typical of conventional forms of change management or professional training.

The "Three Fs" follow a mechanistic logic of "If... then": They are symptomatic of the attempt to tackle a complex problem - learning and change - with complicated means. The notion of the "hero leader as a role model" is based on the same error.

{ If the "Three Fs" worked, then courses and training would be the solution. }

Leadership as social process: Complex, but at least real

There is another, more effective approach to personal change and development.

How to create appropriate conditions for learning with the "Three Rs":

Relate: Establish a relationship. People want to link up, connect to a person or a group, someone who embodies the change positively, or believes in it.

Repeat: Assure repetition. Without this, learning is not possible. New behaviors and skills need to be seriously trained, practiced with discipline, and deepened. In real life.

Reframe: Ensure re-interpretation of present challenges, so that new ways of thinking can emerge and assert themselves. Then, Internalized, congruent new action is possible.

Leadership in the sense of the "Three Rs" operates by influencing people and their contexts, systemically, taking into account both human individuality and value creation structure. Only tending to this process can lead to real results. Leadership that takes complexity into account has less to do with the personality of the individual leader, and more with leadership as a social process. The "Three Rs" do not take responsibility away from "leadership workers." But they make leadership work much more challenging, as they respond to the fact that learning and development are not trivial, but rather complex by nature.

{ One cannot, at the same time, lead and exercise hierarchical power. In complexity, leadership as a social process, as a system's capability, gains prominence. }

Focus leadership work on the system. Not on individual people.

Self-organization in complex systems is natural. Having "a leader" is not. Containing boundary and external markets being in place, this provides for the steering.

Leadership must be work focused on improving the system, on making the market palpable inside the organization. This is done through transparency and dialogue, and by allowing self-organization and social pressure to function.

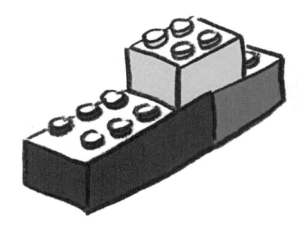

{ Understood correctly, leadership in complexity means working the system, not the people. }

Promote a result-based achievement culture

Make team performance visible - results only, not inputs! - to nurture a team-based "winning culture."

Never, ever, attempt to manage individual performance, though, because individual performance simply does not exist. Stop managing working time or controlling individual behavior - "behaviorism" has been proven counter-productive a long time ago, as it stifles self-organization.

What works, instead: The most adaptive and successful organizations focus on nurturing a culture that highlights the importance of "everybody having fun, while we are winning in the marketplace, together."

You cannot have that, while at the same time controlling people's behavior.

Redefining success for an age of complexity: Why and how to make peace between stakeholder groups

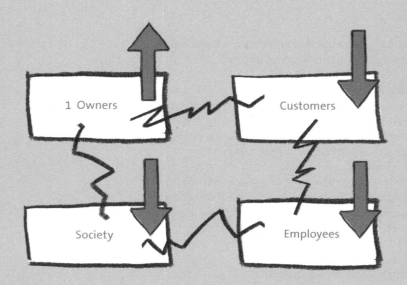

Alpha belief:

"The various stakeholders of an organization are doomed to be in eternal conflict with each other. Therefore, in any given situation, we must give precedence to one particular stakeholder group over the other. When in doubt, these are the owners or shareholders. Sometimes, we will put customers first. Or so we say, anyway. Success is when maximum short-term profit or shareholder value are created."

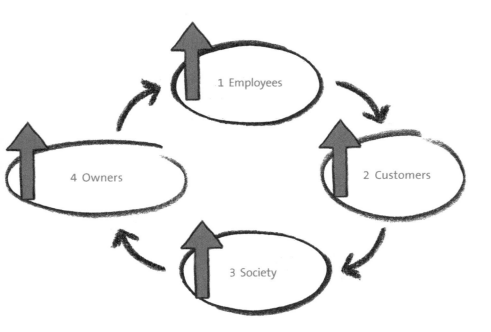

Beta belief:

"The interests of stakeholders are intertwined and interdependent: Success ensues when a virtuous cycle between the value creation for employees, customers, society and owners is produced. This cycle can only begin with the members of the organization - value creation starts with them. They must come first. The cycle must not be broken at the expense of one group or another. Success is when sustainably superior value for all stakeholders is created."

{ Profit maximization and shareholder value theories are mechanistic and, ultimately, anti-social dogmas. Success is not a zero-sum game. And neither is it just "win-win." }

Leadership is:
To influence informal structure

Informal structures can develop a positive force that protects organizations against failure and disorder. A phenomenon such as solidarity, for instance, can only arise out of informal structure.

The first step to effective leadership as influencing informal structure is to recognize it, accept its existence, and create space for it. Do not dismiss it as kitchen chatter! Many of today's leaders do not see themselves as part of informal structure. Or they regard it as illegitimate. This is a mistake.

While informal structure cannot be purposefully molded, and even though most of it eludes direct observation, it can still be "constructively stimulated". Who is part of a system, or allowed in, will influence social structure significantly, as do consciously cultivated rituals. To make information available for all, rapidly and uniformly, i.e. to promote maximum transparency, is an often underestimated factor. Also the creation of great work environments and workplaces for all - something Google proved to be possible.

To foster Informal knowledge forums, "master lodges", leagues, guilds and Communities of Practice (instead of holding the usual conferences and frontal events) is another lever. Far more effective than personnel development is to curate learning processes in which self-awareness, awareness of others, of communication and team effectiveness are increased.

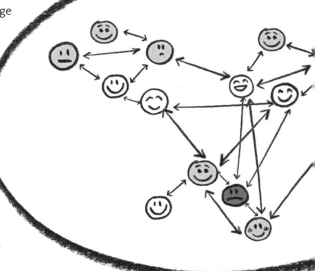

Leadership is:
To influence value creation structure

Leadership does not set targets, nor does it build crash barriers. That is management, or leadership as a position. But leadership is a role, a kind of work, not a job. This work consists of collective action to create a space, a sphere of activity, in which value creation can materialize. Leadership is like creating spaces bounded by cell membranes in which individuals and teams can act as entrepreneurs. With each other and for each other. Strings connect teams. There is nothing locked, or fixed.

Leadership in Beta is no longer synonymous with the right to make decisions. Instead, decision-making power "jumps" to where the problems are: Any decision should be taken by a matching professional, or master.

What, then, remains for "managers" to do? To organize joint action on the sphere of activity, on principles, business and organizational models. To organize "Identity work." To represent externally and to attract the right people. To agilize relationships between cells. To facilitate conflicts. To enable visibility of results. To ensure presence of skill and mastery, without claiming formal power.

If you let formal structure interfere negatively with value creation, you are not doing your job.

{ Leadership takes place in two structures. And, in turn, it alters these structures. }

Recruiting and selection as key leadership disciplines: Get the right people on board

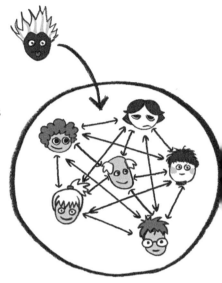

Over the decades, entire selection and assessment industries have emerged. In complexity, they become part of the problem. Highly formalized, standardized, de-socialized processes of selection and promotion have become the rule. Managers and HR professionals share recruitment responsibility among themselves, sometimes supported by assessment psychologists. This leads to an overemphasis of seemingly objective, easily observable selection criteria - in particular behaviors, "skills" and competencies.

Once behavioral standardization and individual competencies become dominant in selection and promotion, low diversity is an inevitable consequence, as well as a chronic lack of cultural "fit" between new entrants and their teams. It is likely that a hierarchy of incompetence will emerge ("As a safeguard, I ensure that people under me are slightly worse than myself").

In Beta, recruiting is seen as the "most sacred" leadership task of all. Here, to be intensively involved in selection is a matter of honor. This results in socially dense selection processes: Colleagues recruit colleagues. Instead of representatives of the formal structure, peers from the informal and the value creation structures will be responsible for selection decisions for their teams. Low formalization and strong dialogue lend weight to less easily observable factors such as "attitude", "cultural fit" and "fit with the team" in the decision-making process. Numerous people (eg, five, eight or more) will be involved in any selection process, and each participant will have the power to eliminate or exclude candidates from a process, if justified.

{ Recruiting and promotion are key business decisions.
A hallmark of great selection is that it is highly time-consuming. }

Promote self-development and mastery

You cannot and need not develop people. People can do this on their own. An organization can and should, however, create conditions and forums for self-development, and it can also ensure that leaders get out of the way by not trying to control or contain self-development.

Individual mastery is the only viable problem-solving mechanism in complexity.

We tend to overrate talent, and underrate systematic, disciplined learning. We tend to overrate classroom training, and underrate learning that is integrated into the actual work life. We tend to overrate formal instruction and underrate inspirational interaction, informal networking and communities of practice.

{ Training budgets only serve to control – not for learning. Scrap them and make learning resources available to those who want to learn, when they want to learn. }

Practice "radical" transparency

Information is to entrepreneurial responsibility
what oxygen is to the human body.
In an organization, without fast and easy access to
information – including that on team performance
and financial results of the organization – teams
and individuals will be walking around in darkness.
Transparency is like turning the light on.

Transparency makes ambition, a healthy spirit
of competitiveness, and group or peer pressure,
possible.

Having "open books" is part of that. If you find
yourself thinking about possible "dangers" of open-
ing the books, then you probably haven't thought
the topic through, yet. In that case, it's time to do
that, now.

Make targets, measures and compensation "relative"

Design principle *Beta:*
- Transparency & Improvement
- Peer (team) comparisons
- Comparisons w/previous periods
- Dialogue & dissent
- Pay by market value
- Profit sharing, gain sharing
- Joint fight against waste
- Target Costing

Design principle *Alpha:*
- Fixed & individual targets
- Management by Objectives
- Budgets & Plans
- Performance Appraisals
- Pay by Position
- Pay for Performance
- Incentives & Bonuses
- Cost Management

In dynamic markets, prognosis becomes impossible.
Planning turns into a futile, if not misleading ritual.

In knowledge-intensive work, dangling carrots in front of people not only fails to work, it actually de-motivates people, strangling engagement and team spirit. Direction via targets, performance measurement, and compensation systems all need to take into consideration complexity, interdependence, and the nature of motivation.

{ Let purpose drive behavior. Not numbers, or manipulative and controlling processes. }

A better way of making decisions in complexity

Consistently decentralized decision-making in a network structure makes having social "glue" between different actors and teams indispensable. Consultation or consultative decision-making is one such means. It is better, still, to elevate consultative individual decision-making to a principle.

As we saw, hierarchical decision-making ("approval by bosses") is not effective in complexity. The obvious and well-known alternatives, such as unanimity or majority decision in committees and meetings, are neither efficient nor practical: they tend to fuel bureaucracy and waste. Dynamic-robust network organizations need more efficient decision-making mechanisms than that.

Consultation generally refers to the collection of information and advice, before making a decision. Physicians, under certain conditions, are obliged to consult with peers. Lawyers are used to this as well.

In organizations with consistently decentralized decision-making, the practice and principle of consultation can also be found. They might call it advice process (AES), deliberation (dm-drogerie markt), recommendation, "waterline" (W.L.Gore) or "nemawashi" (Toyota and others).

{ What distinguishes consultation from dialog: it starts with a specific problem, or decision case; in consultation, exactly one decision-maker (to be nominated on the outset) decides; consultation is not voluntary - it is mandatory. }

This is how "consultative individual decision-making" works

1 Group: "Who is the decision-maker?" Follows the assumption that "bosses should decide as little themselves as possible"; sharpens the problem; chooses decision-maker, applying criteria such as: involvement, proximity to problem, idea scouting quality, ...

2 Decision-maker: "Who do I consult?" Knows that consultation is a duty, not an option; looks for help with those most appropriate: colleagues, internal specialists, external experts, consultants, manager (and, depending on relevance, additionally, the board); is responsible for selecting internal/external consultation partners

3 Decision-maker and the consulted: "What are the options?" Perform "consultative dialogues"; share knowledge; generate ideas; narrow down the decision field; learn from each other and "change" together

4 Decision-maker: "What is my choice?" Takes full responsibility; chooses best option, taking into account different ideas and views; follows up on consequences of the decision; if necessary, defends the decision or modifies it later

5 Group: "What can we do better?" Jointly stands behind the decision, without undermining individual responsibility; celebrates together, gives feedback; "exercises forgiveness", if necessary; later recalls the experience in similar situations

{ Consultation is like a suggestion scheme turned upside-down. }

From Alpha to the BetaCodex and to a set of design principles for complexity-robust organization

	Law	Beta		Alpha
§1	Freedom to act	Connectedness	not	Dependency
§2	Responsibility	Cells	not	Departments
§3	Governance	Leadership	not	Management
§4	Performance climate	Results culture	not	Duty fulfillment
§5	Success	Fit	not	Maximization
§6	Transparency	Flow of intelligence	not	Power accumulation
§7	Orientation	Relative Targets	not	Top-down prescription
§8	Recognition	Sharing	not	Incentives
§9	Mental presence	Preparedness	not	Planning
§10	Decision-making	Consequence	not	Bureaucracy
§11	Resource usage	Purpose-driven	not	Status-oriented
§12	Coordination	Market dynamics	not	Commands

{ Both Alpha and Beta are mindsets based on codices that consist of interdependent sets of laws. In today's dynamics (and with Theory Y people on board), Beta practice will result in superior competitive performance. }

Part 7

Transform, or remain stuck:
The way forward

(How deep organizational
transformation works. Really.)

Transforming organizational models: necessity and challenge

Although tayloristic management or "Alpha" has remained something like the standard model of organizational governance to date, it is nevertheless just the model of the past: As we have seen, the world has already changed - high complexity in value creation has become the norm.

For each existing, older organization, this poses the question: Can we transform ourselves? Or do we actually need to do so? And if so, how one get from Alpha to Beta?

For younger organizations, the question is: How can we avoid or bypass Alpha – and retain a highly entrepreneurial organizational model?

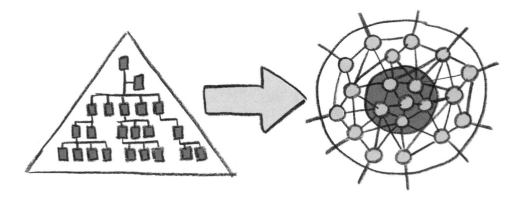

{ Optimization, improving the existing model, "management innovation", or working in the model will not take you from Alpha to Beta. Only working on the model can do this. }

How our understanding of "organizational change" evolved

A helpful model for distinguishing change mindsets and approaches to change comes from Marvin Weisbord. He shows that there are four fundamentally distinct attitudes toward organizational change that have evolved in the last hundred years. The necessary change methods and tools evolved in parallel with these thought models, successively, and in specific historical contexts.

For transformation toward Beta, only the last approach shown here is sufficient: systemic work, organized as a social process.

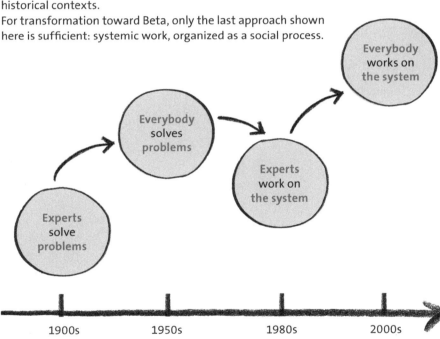

The technology for acting on transformational change as a "collective social process affecting the system" is fairly recent: it has evolved and matured only in the last few decades.

Evolutionary theory for orgs: Transformation is part of organizational normality

Organizations are not born in Alpha mode. They evolve into it or transform to it.

Economist Friedrich Glasl explains this phenomenon in his theory of developmental phases through which an organization can evolve. Borrowing from that, there are three phases or organizational evolution, and three types of transformation.

Alpha is, in this sense, a typical evolutionary step that organizations make. Only very few companies have so far managed to avoid the stage of "Differentiation" entirely.

{ Alpha is a common, but not an inevitable, developmental stage in the life of an organization. }

**Degree of
decentralization
of decision-making**

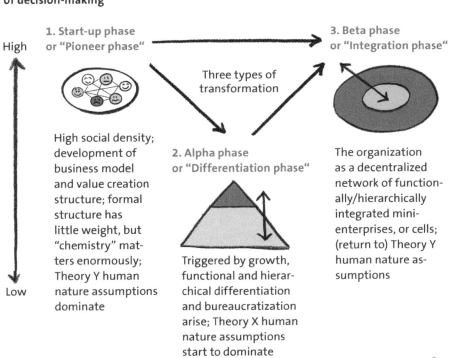

1. Start-up phase
or "Pioneer phase"

High

3. Beta phase
or "Integration phase"

Three types of
transformation

High social density;
development of
business model
and value creation
structure; formal
structure has
little weight, but
"chemistry" mat-
ters enormously;
Theory Y human
nature assumptions
dominate

Low

2. Alpha phase
or "Differentiation phase"

Triggered by growth,
functional and hierar-
chical differentiation
and bureaucratization
arise; Theory X human
nature assumptions
start to dominate

The organization
as a decentralized
network of function-
ally/hierarchically
integrated mini-
enterprises, or cells;
(return to) Theory Y
human nature as-
sumptions

Foundation   Young organization   Older organization   **time**

The three types of transformation: How organizations become "Alpha" - and how they can leave it behind

{ Most organizations have already gone through a transformation - or are right in the middle of one. }

We call the three kinds of organizational transformation "Bureaucratization", "Deepening" and "Beta Transformation."

As centralized steering becomes a problem in complexity, younger, growing companies must learn how to do Deepening - and need to find a way to avoid the Alpha phase.

Almost all larger, older organizations need Beta Transformation - meaning functional and hierarchical integration, combined with decentralization of decision-making.

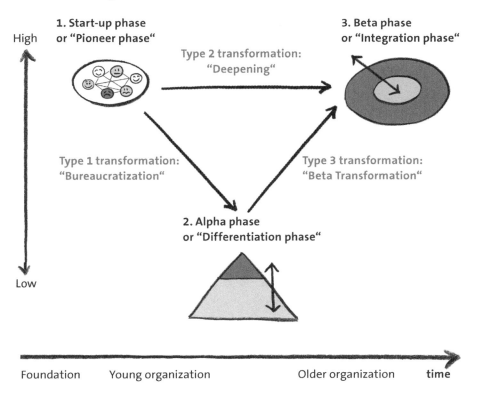

**Degree of
decentralization
of decision-making**

**1. Start-up phase
or "Pioneer phase"**

High

Type 2 transformation:
"Deepening"

**3. Beta phase
or "Integration phase"**

Type 1 transformation:
"Bureaucratization"

Type 3 transformation:
"Beta Transformation"

**2. Alpha phase
or "Differentiation phase"**

Low

Foundation   Young organization   Older organization   **time**

From "awesome start-up" to "ordinary alpha place": the crosswind sensitivity phenomenon

The reason why most organizations today end up in Alpha, or differentiation, phase is called crosswind sensitivity.

Start-ups are "naive Beta organizations." They rarely have a precise understanding of what makes them successful. Consequently, they tend to attribute their success and high performance to their products, or a seemingly superior business model.

Sooner or later, however, every successful, growing start-up is broken down into center and periphery by external dynamics. It reacts to this by either developing hierarchy and functional differentiation - that is the path into the Alpha phase. Or by deepening their Beta organization model, through successive cell divisions.

Bureaucratization tends to happen by surprise. Just as a strong gust of crosswind coming seemingly out of nowhere can knock over a cyclist. The trigger for this transformation is the organization's own growth and subsequent diminishing of social density, but crises also plays a role. Suddenly, the cry for "professionalization" gets voiced: alien best practices are copied, consultants brought in, processes and rules established, formal structures drawn up to oppose the "chaos." Thus, Alpha principles and beliefs are being adopted.
Everybody else is doing it, so why shouldn't we?

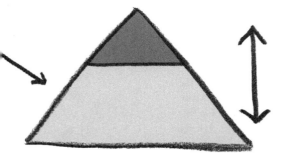

Beta transformation, by contrast, can be pursued only with a high level of collective self-awareness. There are reasons for this. Until today, Alpha is the default organizational model: Alpha repertoire can be learned and practiced practically everywhere. In addition, the collective unconscious is still predominantly shaped by pre-democratic ideas: but Beta requires dealing with power and communication at a higher level of complexity. This is often not internalized, it is not built into the reflexes.

{ Alpha is favored by crosswind sensitivity. Beta is not. }

Steps into Deepening and Beta Transformation: First, make the Sense of Urgency tangible

A Sense of Urgency is the emotional realization that immediate joint action is necessary.
Emotional. Immediately. Together.
Most organizations have never deliberately driven change in a way that is based on these principles.

As we have seen from the "Three Fs" and "Three Rs", if you want to instill change it is not sufficient to show what needs to be done, to get the facts right, or to explain that the status quo is terrible. It is also nonsense to claim that (only) crisis triggers change. To build momentum and energy for change, people must also be convinced that a better future is possible. This has little in common with knowledge, pleas or "solutions."

Do not look for answers at first. Refrain from assigning surveys, or reports. Do not reduce the need for change to cost savings. Instead, try to grasp the core problem emotionally. And show everyone why the change cannot be delayed. Why it cannot be conducted from behind closed doors, nor delivered by top management or consultants alone.

You will notice that you are on the right track to articulating the sense of urgency, when words like "we", "now" and "together" come into play. When you are prepared to formulate the sense of urgency figuratively.

{ A sense of urgency is more than talking about facts. }

Second: Find and unite the core group to become a "guiding coalition" for change

A social group or organization of any significant size has a core group: a group of members "that really matter." This group is an element of informal structure. In order for transformation to happen, the core group - or a relevant part of it - must band together, and take on the leadership of the change process. Alternatively, a new, modified core group can pull together to lead through the change, forming a pact for change with one another.

Change guru John Kotter described the process of formation of such a core group in several of his books, including the fable "Our Iceberg is Melting." Kotter calls the core group for change the "guiding coalition."

The coalition must incorporate diversity. Different levels of formal power and informal influence; different roles, different preferences, different characters and communicative strengths. Only with diversity, and by positively complementing each other, will the core group be able to use the whole gamut of possible transformational interventions and master the challenges and crises in transformation.

{ Every organization already has a core group. For Beta Transformation, this group must unite and learn to lead complex change. The group must become a team. }

Thirdly: Write your organization a letter

As a safeguard against crosswind and as a tool for transformation, self-description is recommended. Self-description as a way of putting the sense of urgency into writing is the most effective vehicle to organize the thought and communication work necessary for profound change. It is an ideal foundation for robust transformation processes.

We call such a self-description the "Letter To Ourselves." You may also call the letter a "manifesto", the "constitution", "charter", or "case for change" for your company. Any organization beyond the start-up phase should produce such a document at some point.

A Letter To Ourselves might have a length of 20 to 40 pages. It can be designed in the form of a small book. The letter is about spelling out why the change is urgent now. Where the organization comes from. And what a better future might look like for it. The letter therefore will always describe the past, present and future.

{ By the way: an organization cannot fully know itself. Therefore, a self-description can only be developed with outside help. }

Fourth: Go with the change energy, not against it. Learn how to confront the two forms of resistance

Organizational transformation as a social process thrives on being operated jointly by all the members of the organization. Not driven by committee, or from behind closed doors. Not from the top down. Not by external specialists. For this to succeed, the formal decision for transformation has to be made as late as possible. It should only take place when virtually all are on board: they resonate with the sense of urgency and relate to the Letter To Ourselves.

Transformation can be neither planned, nor programmed. It requires space for emergence. Therefore, such a process lives from the resonance it itself generates within the organization.

Resistance in transformation is natural. There has to be resistance: Otherwise, the organization would already have been transformed all by itself or as if by magic. In the emergent approach to change described here, resistance is much less broad and less diffuse than is typical in planned change. Two basic forms of resistance are relevant here, however, and both require consistent action and consequence.

The first type is guided by self-interest. We call it tactical resistance. It is relatively scarce. The second is guided by fear of the future and feelings of insecurity. We call it intuitive resistance. The latter can be processed and solved using the "Three Rs." The former cannot.

{ Resistance to change is as natural as sweating is in professional sports. With an emergent approach to change, resistance gets minimized and workable. }

105

Transformation:
A "double helix" process

A process model for changing teams or the organization as a whole can not cope with the full challenge of a Beta transformation. There is another, a second dimension to change: one that is not related to the organization as a social organism, but that has to do with each individual's transformation journey.

Everyone's communication styles and behavior patterns must change. Thus, to achieve true organizational transformation, another dimension needs to be added to the framework: a process model for personal, or individual change.

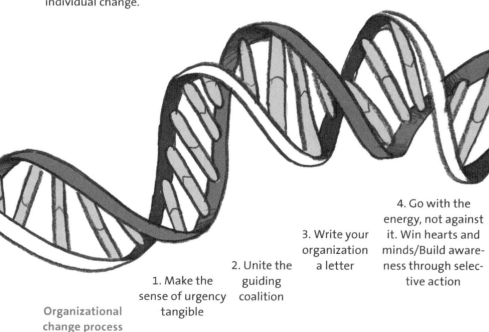

4. Go with the energy, not against it. Win hearts and minds/Build awareness through selective action

3. Write your organization a letter

2. Unite the guiding coalition

1. Make the sense of urgency tangible

Organizational change process

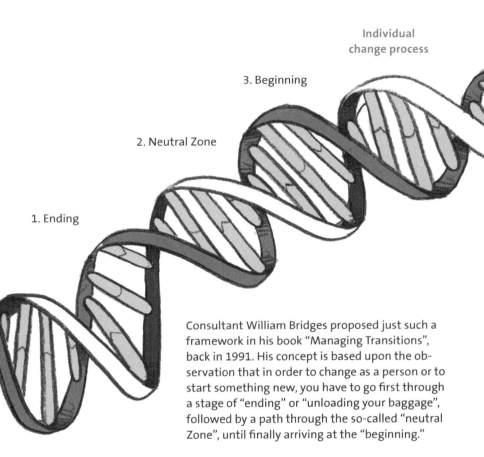

Individual
change process

3. Beginning

2. Neutral Zone

1. Ending

Consultant William Bridges proposed just such a framework in his book "Managing Transitions", back in 1991. His concept is based upon the observation that in order to change as a person or to start something new, you have to go first through a stage of "ending" or "unloading your baggage", followed by a path through the so-called "neutral Zone", until finally arriving at the "beginning."

By combining this with the framework outlined on the previous pages, a completely new kind of change initiative framework emerges. One in which the two different dimensions of profound change – organizational and personal – are intertwined and inseparable. A double helix framework for transformation. It allows for a far richer and more "realistic" perception of profound change processes.

{ Transformation is systemic, dual and coupled by nature.
It eludes project management. It can, however, be led and guided, and supported by method. }

You want to get going?
What your personal influence
really looks like - and how to use it

The Influence Speedometer is a thinking tool that can help to gain a better understanding of your personal influence within you own organization.

Ask yourself: What power do I have? What and who can I influence directly - or indirectly, by "playing over gang"? What speed of change can I expect when I use this influence?

My area of indirect influence:
low to medium
change velocity

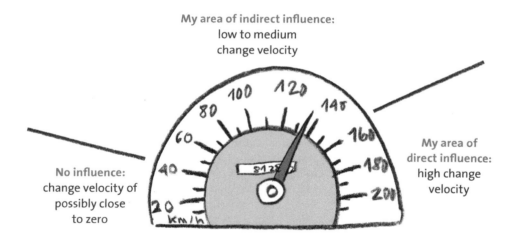

No influence:
change velocity of
possibly close
to zero

My area of
direct influence:
high change
velocity

{ Not to have any influence over one´s own organization is
the exception, not the rule. It is almost always necessary to
"play the ball on the rebound." }

How to nudge your organization onto the path to transformation

Many of us feel helpless in the face of the challenge that profound change poses for an organization. However, there are three things that anyone can do to gently nudge their own organization toward the path of complexity-robustness.

Encourage constructive dialogue and networking. You are a member of the informal structure of your organization. Take advantage of this structure for the purpose of transformation. You will find that you are not alone!

Use existing forums for impulses. Every organization creates communication forums that may be harnessed or "re-purposed" for transformational stimuli. These can be events and conferences, annual gatherings, executive meetings and even Christmas parties. Who are the curators of these forums?

2. How can they help? How do I get in touch?

1. Who?

1. Who?

People with abilities

People with influence

People who appreciate me

1. Who?

Remove what hinders. It is often easier and requires less influence to clear internal obstacles than to implement something completely "new." This does not mean that such organizational hygiene would be less effective than creating new practices.

How to use the search tool. Always answer the Who? question first: Who are those with relevant influence? Those who appreciate me? Those with relevant skills for change? Then comes the How?: How can these actors provide specific help? How can I contact them?

Beta versus Alpha:
The two models, compared

Beta
Alive
Surprise
Principles
Value Creation structure/Flow
Theory Y human nature assumptions
Systemic
Decentralized
Economies of Flow
Technology: Leadership

Network cells as "mini enterprises"
Outside-in value creation relationships/Pull
Stakeholders form a virtuous circle
People first, customers second
"Market" (external reference) is in charge
Functional integration determines structure
Informal structure: cultivated, has space
Leadership: decentralized, temporary
Those who lead serve teams & the whole
Everyone makes important decisions
Consultation gives stability, is mandatory
Complexity-robust: elegant, better & cheaper
Fitting, best quality & cost
The whole is the sum of the interactions
Decide as late as possible
Just-in-time resources, dialog
Teams hire new colleagues
Team-based, self-organization, social pressure
Radical transparency
Relative performance contracts, external referen
Actual-Actual comparisons
Everyone thinks and acts, always
Result sharing & ownership enable connectedne
Celebrate joint success and failure
Pay the person
Agile, Scrum, rapid prototyping, design thinking
Improve interaction, invest in live teams
d continuous

Alpha
Dead
Repetition
Rules
Formal structure/Command
Theory X human nature assumptions
Mechanistic
Centralized
Economies of Scale
Technology: Management

Functions, departments, divisions
Top-Down power relationships/Push
Stakeholder interests in eternal conflict
Customers first! Shareholders first! Profit!
"Management" (internal function) is in charge
Functional division determines structure
Informal structure: repressed
Leadership: centralized, linked to position
Bosses govern by command-and-control
Managers: paid for making decisions
Processes provide stability, must be followed
Efficient: fully utilized, faster & cheaper
More, bigger, market share
The whole is the sum of the parts
Decide as early as possible
Lined-up resources, budgeting
HR and bosses make hiring decisions
Individualizing, hierarchical control, bureaucracy
Information is power
Fixed, internally negotiated performance contracts
Planned-Actual comparisons
Strategic versus operational
Incentives & bonus systems drive performance
Reward & Punish
Pay by position
Project management, Waterfall
Train the individual, personnel development
Change is a controlled and temporary activity
Chasing best practices

Bonus chapter

"Management is Quackery."

(An Interview)

"Management is Quackery."
An Interview

The interview was conducted by Winfried Kretschmer and Michael Kres

Mr. Pflaeging, you advocate doing away with management. Isn't that a pretty bold proposition? Wouldn't it also suffice to just *improve* management?
If you look at larger or even smaller companies, it's clear that more often than not these places have little to offer in terms of quality of life or quality of work. There are good reasons why many people are dissatisfied with their working conditions. There's the famous mental resignation, which is a reaction to the shortcomings in organizations. People are leaving corporations, larger and smaller firms in droves and opting for self-employment. In my view, this distress in organizations, in work, has a single origin, namely the fact that we still attempt to govern work with command-and-control techniques and method, i.e. "managing". We adhere to a dogma of management that is neither appropriate for the people in organizations, nor for investors, nor for customers, society, or other stakeholders.
Doing away with management is not bold - it is long overdue!

What's wrong with management? What are you criticizing?
Just about everything is wrong with management. Management itself is wrong. I like to compare the current situation with the state of medicine or the healing arts in the European Middle Ages. In our latitudes, at the time, people knew hardly anything about the origin of diseases, the scientific knowledge from antiquity was ignored or had been lost, quacks and charlatans used pre-scientific, frequently solely religiously-inspired methods of treating diseases. In those days a typical form of treatment was bloodletting (phlebotomy) - a technique that did nothing to promote recovery, but which killed a fair portion of the patients. A dreadful thing. In the area of organizational leadership, today we are at a turning point that is similar to the state of medicine prior to the Renaissance: We are still hanging on to quackery. Customers and employees are frequently bled by MBA-trained executives, management consultancies bleed dry entire enterprises. Most managers act to the best of their

knowledge and in good faith. Nevertheless, management is more of an obstacle to organizations, to employees, and the customers, than a source of value creation. Complex problems cannot be solved with the management repertoire. They are only made worse with so-called improvements, optimizations, cost management and reorganizations.

The fact is that almost every aspect of corporate management must change. In organizations of any type we need something that is totally different than what we associate with management today.

What precisely do you mean by "management"?
First of all: Management is not the same thing as leadership. Some management experts view them as equivalent. To ignore this difference means misconstruing the history of corporate management. That´s like calling iPads typewriters! Leadership achieves something that is totally different than what management achieves. Management the social technology from the industrial age can offer something quite specific: It is a conceptual model that is suitable for producing efficiency in repetitive, standardized, complicated work. So it is useful under specific conditions: when it is possible to employ the principle of dividing the thinking from the doing. This basic idea goes back to Frederick W. Taylor and it has shaped our society like only a few other ideas have - the theory of evolution, for example. Taylor proposed and devised highly effective methods for "liberating" large parts of the industrial work, at that time still in its infancy, from the thinking; for turning a large share of workers into quasi-machines that would not have to think anymore, but only execute. A century ago this was a truly revolutionary idea. It promised a quantum leap for industrial value creation. Basically, a great thing. The personnel, temporal, and also geographical separation of thinking from acting became the defining principle of management. This was its ingenious core - and now it is its fatal weakness. Today the principle of personnel and temporal division, becomes an obstacle in the way of innovation, quality, customer focus, cost-efficiency, and market orientation - and consequently, the effective handling of complexity.

Your argument is: The basic assumptions are wrong, because the world has changed in the more than one hundred years since management came into being. What are these basic assumptions?
The situation in the industrial age was radically different than the situation today. At

that time, companies existed within pre-democratic societies and acted in markets that were oligopolistic or monopolistic, and that were by no means as globalized and competitive as markets are today. Education was patchy at the time and the average worker could hardly read or write. Most companies could thus afford the luxury of forcing their customers and their employees: Forcing the customers to buy and the employees to work. Management the social technology originated in this context: What is trained at business schools today, as well as the prevailing administrative and leadership practices in companies or the practices disseminated by management consultants, all that originated in this age. We are clinging concepts that have little in common with today's scientific insight and with today's market reality.

If I understand correctly you are speaking of two basic assumptions. The first is related to human nature...

Yes, the underlying assumption of management is a specific perception of human nature: According to this concept, in principle, people are fundamentally trying to avoid work and must be forced or seduced to perform. They must be controlled. Taylor's principle of hierarchical division between thinkers and doers is deeply rooted in this theory, and while this principle was effective during the industrial age, unfortunately that has remained the standard way of leading organizations to this very day. Even though we sense that this division can no longer be considered appropriate.

The challenge today is that we must learn to organize work in accordance with totally different market realities. We need the motivation of all members of an organization, we need the entrepreneurial spirit that people inherently possess. We have known that this impulse exists since the motivational research of the 1950s and 1960s. But 90% of management tools, processes and habits are based on a subordinate and superordinate ideology, on this very perfidious view of human nature: We cannot trust the employees, we must force them, incentivize and control them externally, otherwise performance does not occur. Things only work out when managers, when bosses, force, spoon-feed, bribe, etc. their employees and subordinates. This is the handicapping legacy of the industrial age.

And this view of human nature is wrong!

Certainly. People are not lazy and lethargic per se - even if, naturally, they can engage in such behavior, if needed. They do not need to be forced into work. However, this deeply-seated prejudice about people and their relationship to work is what keeps management alive.

Anyone who has ever learned to believe in command-and-control will have great difficulty in seeing the deficiencies of these methods and turning away from them. Externally controlled processes, are an example, that there must be budgets and cost management; that appraisal and employee assessments are good and right and effective; or that management by objectives and incentive systems are necessary to induce performance, No one would favor their spouse or life partner with a yearly employee performance review, along the lines of: "Honey, let's have a little chat

about your key performance indicators, about performance improvement, about your goals for next year!" We don't do this, nor do we believe that such a thing could be somehow "effective". However in companies this seems quite natural to us.

Basic assumption number two is about organizations and their controllability. Do organizations need hierarchy?
The prejudice mentioned above regarding the concept of human nature is also the basis of the assumption that formal hierarchy must inevitably play a major role in organizations. If people were deficient beings, who chronically attempt to get away from their work, then naturally we would need hierarchy to keep the organization under control, in the light of all those people with their flaws and deficiencies.
The second faulty basic assumption, however, has to do with the illusion of control - the belief that we can somehow control the future, and an organization´s complexity. This is a silly belief, of course, but look at how most managers spend their time - and at what kind of metaphors are conjured up about organizations. The assertion that companies resemble orchestras is an example. Orchestras and companies have rather little in common, other than the fact that both naturally require a relatively large number of people. Orchestras jointly interpret an existing score, by contrast companies must deal with an uncertain future. They act in markets where they constantly encounter problems that they have never encountered before. By necessity, companies must always venture into something new that they never have encountered before. They are not following a score, they are not interpreting a pre-defined score.
The future is unforeseeable, it is entrepreneurial. However, prevailing management thought is rooted in the dogma that we are able to somehow master the future, and control it: We just need to think of a goal and make a plan of how we can achieve it! The underlying belief is that the future is obedient to our plans, foreseeable, controllable. In reality, of course, markets are highly dynamic and surprising. And the more dynamic and complex markets become, the more internal control and central economic planning drive organizations into the wall.
A few decades ago we all realized that central economic planning is not fit to steer or govern national economies. However we have not yet understood that the same also applies for companies, and for organizations at large. We do not make progress or improve performance with strategic planning, budgeting, target-setting, and fixed guidelines - simply because the future is simply not predictable and organizations

are complex systems. Management is something like Soviet economy for companies. Targets are fixed, incentives are linked to the targets, and overall the attempt is made to have employees under control, so that they follow these plans, quotas, budgets, and objectives. Combined with a total suppression apparatus and fear, wherever necessary. That is soviet at heart. This is Soviet economy - and we call it management!

Wouldn't the gentle coercion that happens once flatter, younger organizations become more effective and more productive, suffice to eradicate management, over time? Or do we need something like a revolution in existing companies?
I do not believe that "gentle coercion" is a change approach capable of triggering the needed transformational effect in organizations around the world. Management is a mindset that will not just go away all by itself. We all carry mental models that make it possible for us as human beings to survive at all in a complex environment. And we have learned to solve problems in a specific manner, to work together in organizations in a specific manner. If we now want to change that, because the old methods no longer work, then we are confronted with the problem of how to generate collective learning.
If the mental "management" model is no longer helpful, then first of all, this means that we must accept this fact, and then we must change our thinking. We must all unlearn and learn new things. This acknowledgement is still quite uncommon, however. On the organizational level, this amounts to a leadership revolution indeed. But on the individual level, this does not require a revolution, rather it requires a learning process, a variety of learning steps, at the end of which a person notices that he or she thinks differently and can now access other, more effective behavioral repertoires.
One of my consulting clients described this individual transformation process like this: A person in this learning phase would frequently experience flashes of insight, i.e. somewhat abrupt moments of knowledge, in which new, more effective behavioral possibilities open up. However, between these encouraging flashes of insight the person also would experience continuous relapses into old behavioral patterns - which in turn can feel somewhat disheartening.
Thus we better find a different path than just hoping for external pressure or stimulus to make the change happen for us. We better look for ways to generate these flash moments and increase their frequency. In this regard, the fact that there are quite a few pioneering organizations that have already been down this path, is of help, but it is not sufficient. There are a fair amount of examples of organizations that have transformed themselves, or that have maintained a "beta" organizational model throughout their existence, and from which one can learn. But transformation within an existing organization also requires method.

How long do you give the existing central economic structures in companies?
It is incumbent on the power of the markets, to determine how long the individual companies that pursue the dogma of management, or command-and-control, will

still be able to survive. Ultimately, the markets will put an end to management as we know it today. In some industries this displacement process is already well underway, for example in the global automotive industry. Or take the German drugstore market, where the former market leader, Schlecker, was swept out of the market through pressure from un-managed competitors, such as dm-drogerie markt, The old organizational model causes its own demise. After 100 years of management, we are approaching a generational change in the paradigms of organizational leadership. A renaissance of work and organizations.

You once worked as a financial controller yourself and experienced major corporations first-hand. At that time, what was the key experience that sparked your conviction that management is superfluous?
Basically there were two types of key experiences. On one hand, as a finance manager I had a substantial aha moment. After several years in the business I simply couldn't help but notice that instruments and methods, such as budget planning, strategy, management reporting, forecasting – namely the entire planning and reporting system – do not work. Common performance management systems, overall, including those bits overseen by human resources areas, produce neither alignment, nor efficiency, nor insight, nor dialogue. Not to mention improvement! They only produced inertia, fatigue and demotivation.
In addition there was the personal experience with bosses and executives through which I noticed the many different ways in which hierarchical direction and control regularly failed. This notion that bosses must always know and always be in charge, that they can make better decisions than their underlings – that didn't work out at all, regardless of where I looked and whom I listened to.
Today, in my role as a consultant, I continue to observe that communication in organizations almost everywhere takes place in a manner that is too one-sided and that rarely puts people on an equal footing. Particularly when people and teams get under pressure, which of course is highly common. Consequently, there is a lack of learning, a lack of space for developing mastery, and a lack of space for social corrective mechanisms. The right thing, the sensible thing, usually can not force its way through. This command-and-control failure can be observed practically everywhere, in all kinds of organizations. We all know and recognize the symptoms. That´s why books such as "How to work for an idiot" or "The no asshole rule" are best-sellers.

What happens when management is done away with? Does total chaos break out? What does that mean for the managers?

To put management on the garbage heap of history, we do not need to send managers to the block! The issue is really not to get rid of managers, but rather to abolish management the technology. Think about what happens to the typewriters: No one needs a typewriter anymore. We are all still writing, maybe more than ever before – however we are writing with PCs, laptops, tablets, mobile phones, all kinds of gadgets. The crucial change associated with the transition from management to more contemporary, complexity-robust organization consists of abolishing the division between those who think and those who act: In such an organization, all will be permitted to think, can think, and they are suddenly are expected to think at all times. This is decidedly fraught with consequences and is not so easy to imagine for most people within today's enterprises with their rituals, dogmas, processes, rules, and management tools!

In the new dogma it is not just a few managers who think, there are perhaps thousands of people who are thinking. In such an organization the need for transparency and genuine team coordination - not coordination through bosses - develops quite quickly. Greater social density occurs, as does more constructive group pressure. More collective intelligence, more self-organization, more dissent.

But there must be someone who has the overall vision - the big picture.

Many in an organization should see the big picture, ideally all should have an overall view. But for leaving command-and-control behind, oversight must not be coupled with the power of supervision. With decision-making sovereignty and power over everything and everyone. In a newspaper editorial office the editor-in-chief, for example, and the managing editor, both oversee. They are ambassadors of the big picture. However, they do not make all the decisions. Quite the contrary. And in daily editorial meetings everyone, really everyone is expected to or condemned to think for themselves.

Why do you speak of alpha companies and beta companies?

At first glance, the distinction between alpha and beta, between management and actual leadership, may appear somewhat complicated. On the other hand, precise terms and distinctions are needed in the organizational context so that people can think the new and distinguish in from the old at all. This has to do with "branding" - in the original sense of the word: Originally branding referred to the marking of cattle with brand marks that would identify the proprietor. A rancher marked his own cattle in order to differentiate them from the cattle of other ranchers. We need the same concept now in organizations, in companies: For profound change, people need to be able to differentiate what alpha management is, on one hand – i.e. practices, rituals, concepts, dogmas that cause or perpetuate division between thinking and doing. And what beta leadership is, on the other hand. Most companies, managers, and founders are not even aware that there are two distinct models of organizational

leadership. An old one that did a remarkably good job in the industrial age, and a new one that is actually fit for today´s markets and complexity.

In my transformational work during the last decade or so, I noticed that people become better and faster at recognizing, learning and consistently practicing the new mode if they constantly juxtapose this new mode against the old mode. We must learn to see the distinction.

What does this mean, specifically?
An example: About 40 years ago we experienced the so-called third revolution in the automotive industry, which was primarily associated with the rise of Toyota. Many wanted to emulate the success of the Toyota model, which stands for holistic success and the highest efficiency. However: the fact that so-called andon cords (with which the workers could stop the production line single-handedly, if need be, like at Toyota) were successively adopted car factories around the world, did not mean, by any stretch of the imagination, that the Toyota way, Toyota thinking, and Toyota culture had been introduced. In an organization shaped by fear, such lines actually do not make much sense at all, because pulling the ripcord could result in reprisals, and might be viewed as an admission of failure.

Complexity-robust organization such as Toyota´s is simply not a tool. Nor does it come about through tools. It is comprised of a variety of principles, of hundreds of concepts, to which all employees, including executives have to be absolutely committed. That all members of an organization hold firmly in their hearts and minds. In order to create a transformation process towards such a high-performance culture, we must understand what makes the two models of organizational leadership tick: That tayloristic, hierarchical-bureaucratic "alpha" model, optimized for external control. And the beta model, trimmed for self-control, decentralization and shared responsibility. In today's corporate world alpha is still the standard, beta is the exception. Toyota is one of these exceptions – and has been for 50 years. In dynamic, crowded markets, alpha firms cannot cope with the competitive pressure that beta companies exert through their high-performance. However: Only those who are aware of the old can take on the new. More than ever, sustainable high-performance is driven not by the quality of products and services, but by the fitness of organizational models.

How can one tell whether one is dealing with an alpha or a beta organization?

It's quite simple, really – there are many symptoms that are typical for the respective model. For last few years, I've been living in the US part-time, and I often shop there at a grocery store called Trader Joe's. This retail chain belongs to the German Aldi holding, but it´s a bit different than its European counterpart. Each branch looks like it's a local grocery store – in its appearance it reflects the area or neighborhood where it is located. This has a very informal and pleasing effect. Not to mention the high quality of the products and the sensational prices compared to other supermarkets. Now, if you want to find out whether this is a beta company or an alpha company, you usually just need to ask the employees a few questions. Confront them with a problem. In a beta organization, such as Trader Joe's, most of the time you simply get intelligent, thoughtful answers from every employee. At Trader Joe's the employee bears the responsibility and also takes it on. In a beta enterprise no one says: "I'm not responsible for that!", "That's just the way it is around here.", "I can't do anything about it." or: "You can still file a complaint with management!"

However, in beta organizations curious incidents can occur, which elsewhere would almost be inexplicable. Take Southwest Airlines, also a mature beta organizations. A few years ago at Southwest, a flight attendant requested a female passenger to leave the airplane, because he or she considered her skirt to be too short. Too sexy. This woman, in her miniskirt, then toured the US talk shows and caused a little stir with her story about how she had not been treated "properly" by the company and how she had been discriminated. Southwest, however, stood by its principle: Flight attendants make a wide range of decisions for themselves and should always act as though the company belonged to them. Thus when employees think for themselves and make entrepreneurial decisions autonomously, you must at all times bear joint responsibility for those decisions, even if you or other members of the organization might have decided differently.

This is where friction, and learning, and a great deal of collective intelligence occur. At Handelsbanken, a European universal bank headquartered in Sweden they are proud that they do not operate call centers; Handelsbanken believes that people within a call center structure cannot effectively think and act in an entrepreneurial manner. At Handelsbanken, Southwest, or Trader Joe's they would and cannot run annual planning exercises because they do not want to patronize their own people! A "beta" kind of organization produces many such stories: Peculiarities, unusual practices, by which they can be instantly recognized among so many over-managed and under-led organizations.

You have been a close observer of the European drugstore retail chain, dm-drogerie markt, based in Germany. According to you, this is a company that transformed itself into a beta organization about twenty years ago. Tell us more about how this transformation happened.

A story told by Goetz Werner, the company cofounder and principal owner, illustrates the attitude that I call the BetaCodex particularly well. Werner says until the 1980s, he thought that he was a good manager when he was able to give an answer to any employee who would come up with a question. After all, a good boss naturally

knows things better and must be decisive, right? Then Werner recognized that there was a world of difference between this attitude and genuine leadership. He noticed that it would be better if the people who ask him something would not leave his office with ready answers, but rather with five very good, new questions. Employees should not follow! They should work out options and solutions for themselves, take on responsibility, and assess risks. He wanted to bring them into a permanent thinking and learning process. That is the essence of leadership work.

So what does an company like DM look like today, twenty years after the transformation into a beta organization?
A while ago I had the opportunity to participate in an internal DM leadership conference with approximately 200 executives. At the event I found it remarkable, just how high the level of reflection and overall self-awareness is in this company, as compared to other companies that I have become acquainted with in my consulting work. The difference was striking.
In general, one might say that beta organizations produce far more collective discipline and create a place for reason, not obedience. People act altogether more thoughtfully, but also combined with a lot more questioning and dissent. I would paraphrase that with "professional and cultivated". Employees at DM, at Handelsbanken, or Toyota usually have a sensationally clear understanding of what makes them successful jointly, of how value is created, and how performance works.

You associate beta organizations with a concept that you refer to as connectedness. Explain this term to us in more detail.
Basically companies are the coolest adventure playgrounds in the world. They are constantly confronted with a huge number of problems that need to be solved. For intelligent, learning people that is the best breeding ground for excitement, stimulation, intellectual challenge. And also for creating a sense of identity or sense of purpose. Alpha organizations are designed and run in such a manner that they don't even allow all of their employees to get close to the problems. Here, the prevailing paradigm is that problems must be functionally divided, the pieces allocated to functions, and dealt with in a standardized fashion, predictably and in accordance with hierarchic order. This paradigm leads to an incredible waste of challenge, motivation, creative potential and ultimately, enjoyment of work.
Beta organizations approach all of this differently. They confront many, even all

members of the organization with problems. They organize innovation in such a way that ultimately each person shares in it, and can couple his or her motivation to the purpose of the work. Each day and every day. Google and W.L.Gore are notable examples among beta organizations, in this regard. In these companies each employee can and should initiate research and development projects; financial resources are supposed to follow the ideas, not the other way round. Not mechanical allocation and budgets, but people with ideas. This way, people are far more likely to connect with the purpose of the organization.

People hang on to power. How does the issue of power fit in the context of a beta organization?
I'm often asked that question. Probably because we are taken in by the misconception that only a limited amount of power is available in any given organization. In an alpha organization, managers have the power, everyone else is powerless. This is classical taylorism. Now, a popular suspicion is that managers who share power with team members in a beta organization must forfeit some of their power. But power is certainly not a zero-sum game. If I share my power with others, we may gain power overall as a team because we may work together more successfully – and thus ultimately gain influence collectively. Once we start to define power as shared influence on informal structures and value creation, it becomes clear that power in a managed hierarchy is hollow and empty. That´s why often managers in alpha organizations are tragic figures, above all.

Can the beta model also be applied to industries that are less complex?
The more complex the value creation of the organization is, the more the significant the advantages of a beta organization are. We must not equate complexity of products with complexity of value creation, however. Complexity in value creation is now having an effect everywhere, even in traditionally relatively slow-moving industries, such as the insurance industry, or energy.
We have found beta pioneers in all possible industries. With Toyota there is at least one beta automotive manufacturer – this is probably one of the most complex manufacturing industries that exists. There is a bank that has been ticking along for more than 40 years in accordance with the BetaCodex. An airline. Various retail companies, manufacturers of consumer goods and service providers. We found Google, SAS, Valve, and other beta pioneers among Internet and software companies. Or take W.L.Gore, a highly innovative technology company. In the health sector we found DaVita, the US dialysis provider.

Doesn't the beta model potentially privilege the well-educated, those who can establish themselves in a highly professional environment?
Only if you assume that a good education quasi-automatically generates the capacity to think for yourself and to act in a responsible, entrepreneurial manner. But this is likely to be an incorrect assumption. Any pre-school child today has more desire to learn and to take on responsibility than does the usual high-school graduate, who

early-on had this desire and capacity driven out of him or her by our schooling and education system. The higher education systems meander along in the same spirit. In the education system we find precisely the same crippling metal models from the industrial age that we encounter in work and organizations.

Organizations additionally intensify their problems by applying selection and hiring procedures that pay too much attention to technical qualification and experience, instead of attitude, team constellations, and cultural fit. Several beta pioneers, such as Southwest Airlines, turned these assumptions around long ago. At Southwest they rate the attitude and cultural "fit" of job applicants significantly higher than technical qualifications. They consequently stopped hiring people who previously worked as flight attendants at other airlines, as these would often come "spoiled" by the far less entrepreneurial cultures of the competitors. Southwest´s sustained (not-only) economic success over the course of the last four decades in this extremely difficult industry indicates that the company is on the right track.

So how should we imagine the transition from alpha to beta? Who initiates such a change process?
Who initiates the process or who throws the first ball is not so important. However top management must catch the ball and say: "We want to understand, we must figure out why we no longer get our problems solved in the old mode, why our change initiatives are becoming less and less successful, and why our employees appear to be lazy-minded and demotivated." Top management must want to understand why the former path has come to an end, and how an alternative organizational model would work. Then top management must take on the responsibility for the process itself. Simply "supporting" or "endorsing" from a distance does not suffice!

What are the next steps?
There are two paths. On one hand, we have found beta organizations where individuals initiated and drove this kind of transformation. I call such figures "shining lights". Goetz Werner of dm-drogerie markt, Dr. Jan Wallander of Handelsbanken, Taiichi Ohno or Toyota or Ricardo Semler of Semco in Brazil – these are or were such shining lights. They are downright geniuses, who with a lot of energy and charisma initiated far-reaching changes in their organizations. However, they also understood where emphatic action and decisiveness were needed.
Naturally there are only a few such geniuses of change. Shining lights are rare! Thus

in today's organizations, as a rule, we must rely on something else – namely on core groups or guiding coalitions of those who are willing to lead the transformation. Such a guiding coalition will consist of a number of individuals who jointly bring along with them the essential change skills, such as assertiveness, passion, informal influence, formal power, and intellectual caliber. Not in a single person but rather as a team. The American change expert, John Kotter, has described in a crisp and comprehensible manner what such an approach for profound change must look like.

Why don't we see many more beta organizations already?
We have a thinking problem. It is difficult for most people to contemplate organization performance, and success effectively, because their conceptual tools or their "mental models", as Max Weber called them, are shaped by obsolete alpha or management dogmas, and are no longer suitable for solving problems.
It is really no one's fault that alpha thinking, up to this day, remains the standard model of organizational leadership. Let's take a few examples: 90% of risk management consists of methods that don´t reduce, but actually generate and promote risks. Quality management is almost always ineffective. Cost management is consistently ineffective and harmful – it's resembles shadowboxing. Formal structures induce lack of coordination and silo thinking. Compensation systems cause the very problems that they profess to solve. This does not mean that risk, quality and costs, structure, and remuneration are not important. However, the way alpha organizations are dealing with these issues is a little like if we were still treating illnesses today with bloodletting and enemas.
Under the conditions of the industrial age – in sluggish markets and with relatively low-complexity value creation, efficiency gains could be achieved with management methods such as standards, rules, and planning. Even if these methods, even then, were not considered morally unobjectionable. In the meantime these methods have become a problem in a variety of ways – both economically and morally. For most managers it takes some effort to imagine alternatives. An alternative to cost management, for example. Or: What would more effective organizational structures look like, without functional division, and beyond the usual org chart? How do teams improve performance without fixed, set targets, budgets, plan/actual comparisons? How does one lead without making decisions? In all these areas there is a serious need for development and learning.

This means managers, practitioners, don't even know the alternatives that may have already existed for decades?
At least they cannot easily imagine these alternatives within the context of their own organizations, or practically comprehend how these alternatives could be applied to their own problems. Naturally, you can send managers from General Motors, from Fiat, or VW to visit Toyota. All this has been done in the past. It was done 30 or 40 years ago. Managers flew to Japan in droves to take a look at the "Japanese productivity miracle" – primarily to figure out what Toyota did. Most of these managers visited Toyota factories while they were there. What did they learn

there? Not much. More often than not, they simply could not see or understand the model that was explained to them. But to grasp a different kind of thinking is not so easy either. It is almost impossible to describe beta value creation and beta logic by using alpha terminology and language, and with alpha logic in your head.

There is that anecdote of a General Motors manager who had just come back from Japan and who was firmly maintaining that the Japanese had shown his group of visitors "fake" factories – imitations of factories, so to speak. He would also prove it – namely by the fact those supposed factories did not even hold any stock and inventory!

We can say: To this date most organizations have learned little from Toyota and other pioneers of the beta model. They have imitated some of what was obvious. However, they usually have not been able to copy beta thinking - and that is what hey should have learned. And that is not something that you can learn by just watching. If someone went to DM and wanted to describe the leadership model there with standard management vocabulary, or assign the practices at DM to classic management tools, he or she would inevitably fail.

How do you judge the capacity for rethinking, in organizations?
Again and again I experience managers who quite quickly succeed in thinking themselves into the BetaCodex. A few years ago I was invited to meet with top executives from an Italian banking group with around 10,000 employees. I explained the BetaCodex and Handelsbanken´s organizational model to the CEO and his team. The CEO was a very objective, rational, thoughtful man. He listened attentively, however he did not say much. So, during the entire meeting I was not sure of what he thought about the matter.

After one and half hours he said: "Now I understand the Handelsbanken model. This is precisely the philosophy that we need, but that we do not have today, and that is so infinitely difficult for us to grasp." Then he said: "With regards to some technical issues of our industry I simply cannot yet imagine how these can be solved in the beta mode. However: If Handelsbanken does practice this successfully, then most likely there must be alternative solutions out there for these technical issues." In other words he had immediately started to think himself into this new logic that was still very strange to him.

Without this willingness to learn how to solve problems differently, with a new kind of thinking, transformation is not possible.

The rest

For digging deeper

(How to continue the journey)

Recommended reading

Haeckel, Stephan: Adaptive Enterprise – Creating and Leading Sense-And-Respond Organizations. HBRP, 1999

Kleiner, Art: The Age of Heretics: A History of the Radical Thinkers Who Reinvented Corporate Management. Jossey-Bass, 2nd edition, 2008

Kotter, John: Leading Change. HBRP, 1996

Kotter, John/Rathgeber, Holger: Our Iceberg is Melting – Changing a nd Succeeding Under Any Conditions. St. Martin´s Press, 2006

McGregor, Douglas: The Human Side of Enterprise, annotated edition, McGraw-Hill, 2005

Mintzberg, Henry: Strategy Bites Back - It Is Far More, & Less, Than You Ever Imagined. FT Press, 2004

Morgan, Gareth: Images of Organization. Sage Publications, updated edition, 2006

Pasmore, Bill: Creating Strategic Change - Designing the Flexible, High-Performing Organization. Wiley, 1994

Peters, Tom: Re-Imagine! Business Excellence in a Disruptive Age. DK Publishing, 2003

Pflaeging, Niels: Heroes of Leadership - The Men and Women Who Advanced Organizational Thinking in Theory and Practice. BetaCodex Network white paper, 2013

Pflaeging, Niels: Turn Your Company Outside-In! - A Paper on Cell Structure Design. BetaCodex Network white paper, 2012

Purser, Ronald/Cabana, Steven: The Self-Managing Organization – How Leading Companies Are Transforming the Work of Teams for Real Impact. Free Press, 1998

Seddon, John: Freedom from Command and Control – Rethinking Management for Lean Service. Productivity Press, 2005

Weisbord, Marvin: Productive Workplaces – Dignity, Meaning, and Community in the 21st Century, 3rd Edition. Pfeiffer, 2012

Complementary video content

Watch related online video content by the author.

Bonus online content: Additional resources are available on the extras page of this book´s website at: www.organizeforcomplexity.com

About the author

A way to describe myself: I am a consultant, speaker and author living in New York City and Wiesbaden, Germany. I regard myself as a serious business thinker, but also as a practitioner: as an advisor, I help managers and organizations of all kinds to master profound change. For five years, I was a director with the Beyond Budgeting Round Table BBRT, a think tank. Before that, I had worked as a controller at multinational industrial corporations for a few years. During this period, I discovered my passion for organizational transformation, with which I have been engaged full-time since 2003 in a variety of roles. This is my fourth book about this topic, and my first book ever to be published in English. All concepts presented in this book are both research-based and practically tested.

Another way to describe myself: Early-on, I wanted to experience and understand the world. So I looked for opportunities to get to know different cultures and countries, and to work in diverse contexts. I spent one of my college years in Seville, Spain, and later worked in Buenos Aires for a while. I lived in São Paulo for 12 exciting years. Through my work, I found and find opportunities to experience work and life in in many countries, and I got used to working in four languages. All that, I believe, has shaped my view of organizations. Despite differences in language and culture, our handling of work is surprisingly homogeneous, globally, which is probably explained by conditioning during our formative years. Learning and education have consequently become a matter of strong interest to me as well. Since 2011, I have been teaching leadership and high performance in complexity at several universities and colleges. I am a dedicated promoter of and activist for profound reform within business education.

My white papers in English are published on the portal of the BetaCodex Network, a movement I cofounded. You can access the white papers from this page: www. betacodex.org/papers . I look forward to hearing from you. So get in touch, if you like. E-mail: contact@nielspflaeging.com. Follow me on Twitter at @NielsPflaeging

About this book

Organize for Complexity turns out to be quite a distinctive book, compared to
my previous ones. I enjoyed gaining some experience with writing and publishing
books on leadership. Between 2003 and 2011, I wrote three, all in all, among them
"Leading with Flexible Targets" and "Bye-bye Management!", which were published
in German and a few other languages. I am pleased that reviews and feedback
from readers and critics were always predominantly positive and even enthusiastic.
Including a few business book awards.

But I could not help noticing that the ideas on leadership, change and learning
that I endorsed in my books only reached and (more importantly) touched a tiny
fraction of their intended audiences. I wanted my readers to have a similarly in-
tense, fun and engaging experience that I saw audiences having in my workshops,
seminars and keynotes! But that did not quite seem to happen with the books.
The traditional textbook format may convey that kind of experience to some - but
certainly not to everyone.

So with this one, I am trying a fresh approach to the business book. It is designed
to reach "readers" and "non-readers" alike. Those who like words. Those who like
imagery, visuals, color, playfulness, aesthetics. And those who want to experience
fun while learning something useful about business, organizations, and leadership.
This book is designed to be "read" and experienced in greatly varying ways.

Writing, editing and publishing this book felt very different from what I experienced with my other books. It was a much more intimate process: approaching the
work without a traditional publisher gave me full control over all elements of the
book, for the first time. Which was and is truly refreshing, and exciting.

I hope this book will be the start of a journey for you. I hope you enjoy it and that it
will inspire you to act on it!

Thank you

My special thanks go to my maverick companion, collaborator, muse and wife, Silke Hermann. I find traces of her on every page, in every paragraph of this book. She very much shaped the concept of this work and her editorial guidance influenced it at every stage of the project.

Thanks to my "cool friends" and collaborators Valérya Carvalho and Lars Vollmer, who contributed to the project during the concept, manuscript development and review stages.

To graphic designer Pia Steinmann. Without her, bringing this book to life would not have been possible.

To Jurgen Appelo, whose hand-drawings originally inspired me to conceptualize the Organize for Complexity white paper. Jurgen also generously gave me permission to use his illustrations for the early incarnations of the paper.

To my friend and mentor, systems theorist and consultant Gerhard Wohland, for quite a few of the models and thinking tools referred to in this book.

To Deborah Hartmann Preuss and Paul Tolchinsky, who reviewed and transformed the manuscript.

To all my online and offline friends who helped me along the way, including Bill Pasmore, Robin Fraser, Gebhard Borck, Andrej Ruckij, Sergio Mascheretti, Harold Jarche, Jay Cross, Jon Husband, Dawna Jones, Sasha Spencer, Chris Catto and Oliver Gorus.

Personal notes

Personal notes

Personal notes

nielspflaeging.

350 West 42nd Street - 48E | New York, NY 10036 USA
Kirchgasse 22 | D - 65185 Wiesbaden   E-mail: contact@nielspflaeging.com

Version 1.2. - Deming

Lightning Source UK Ltd.
Milton Keynes UK
UKOW07f1026301015

261750UK00008B/20/P

The
RIVERSIDE
READER